DECENTRALISED PLANNING

DECENTRALISED PLANNING

Dr. A.D. Mishra

ABHIJEET PUBLICATIONS
DELHI 110094

ABHIJEET PUBLICATIONS
2/46 Tukhmeerpur Extension
Delhi-110 094
Phone: 011-22960492, 65698474
E-mail: abhijeetpublication@gmail.com

DECENTRALISED PLANNING

First Published 2009

ISBN 978-81-89886-92-9

PRINTED IN INDIA

Published by J.K. Singh for Abhijeet Publications, Delhi-110 094, Lasertypeset by Gaurav Graphics, New Delhi and Printed at Himanshu Printers, Delhi.

Preface

The ideas of "Grass Roots Planning" and "Planning from Below" have the roots in Gandhian Thoughts. The quest of humanity for social justice and sustainability will remain a dream until and unless humanity realizes what Gandhi meant when he said, that economics is untrue which ignores and disregards moral values. In the 22nd July, 1946 issue of *Harijan,* Gandhi stated that 'Independence must begin at the bottom'. Gandhi held that by serving the villages, swaraj could be established. The country's prosperity and progress depends upon the villages. He maintained that if the village perishes, India will perish too. The importance of rural development should be obvious in country where four out of every five citizens live in the countryside. India lives in villages. Unless the socio-economic and political situation of rural India changed, India cannot progress.

Gandhi therefore determined to work for small rural communities wherein people will cooperate with one another and give aid to those who lack the resources for growth and development. He spoke and wrote about village swaraj. He said, "the swaraj of my dreams is the poor man's swaraj. The necessaries of life should be enjoyed by you in common with those enjoyed by the princes and the moneyed men. But that does not mean that you should have palaces like theirs. They are not necessary for happiness. You or I would be lost in them. But you ought to get all the ordinary amenities of life that a rich man enjoys. I have not the slightest doubt that swaraj is not Poorn Swaraj until these amenities are guaranteed to you under it".

Gandhiji found the picture of his free India in its essentials embodied in a song that was sung at one of his evening prayers in Bhangi Colony, New Delhi. What emerged was a picture of the India of his dreams. It was as follows:

We are inhabitants of a country
    where there is no sorrow and no suffering,
Where there is no illusion nor anguish,
    no delusion nor desire,
Where flows the Ganges of love
    and the whole creation is full of joy,
Where all minds flow in one direction,
    and where there is no occasion for sense of time,
All there wants satisfied;
Here all barter is just,
Here all are cast in same mould,
Here is no lack nor care,
No selfishness in any shape or form,
No high no low, no master no slave;
All is light, yet no burning heat,
That country is within you-
    It is Swaraj, Swadeshi,
The home within you-
    Victory! Victory! Victory!
He realizes it who longs for it.

Gandhiji concept of rural development emerge out from what he said in *India of My Dreams*. It Follows:

I shall strive for a constitution, which will release India from all thralldom and patronage, and give her, if need be the right to sin. I shall work for an India, in which the poorest shall feel that it is their country in whose making they have an effective voice; an India in which there shall be no high class and low class of people; an India in which all communities shall live in perfect harmony. There can be no room in such an India for the curse of untouchability or the curse of the intoxicating drinks and drugs. Women will enjoy the same right as men. Since we shall be at peace with all the rest of the world, neither exploiting, nor being exploited, we should have the smallest army imaginable. All interests not in conflict with the interests of the dumb millions will be scrupulously respected, whether foreign or indigenous. Personally, I hate distinction between foreign and indigenous. This is the India of my dreams. ... I shall be satisfied with nothing less.

Gandhi placed rural development at the core of India's future destiny—not rural development visualized microcosmically but in terms of the development of each of its numerous villages to full potential. Gandhi not only expected most of them to continue living in villages but wanted them to do so for to give legitimacy to people's participation.

Revival of the village is indeed the key to the regeneration of India and the fulfillment of the mission in the world, "I want villages to live", says the architect of modern India Pandit Jawahar Lal Nehru, "and I do not care what happens to the towns because I am convinced that if village die, there can be no hope for towns. If villages prosper India is also bound to prosper." In fact, the road to the village is the road to the Heaven of India's soul, the road to the cradle of our civilization, the road to real yagna. The village will be barometer of India's progress and prosperity. "Going back to villages", says Dr. Radhakrishnan, "is not to become primitive". It is the only way to keep us in the mode of existence that is instructive to India, that supplied him once with purpose, a faith and meaning. It is the only way to keep our species civilized."

Decentralised Planning is not as simple as it looks on paper. Capabilities have to be built up, suitable structures have to be valued, changes have to be brought about in the administrative, technical and political arena. Equally important is kindling the zeal and enthusiasm of the people. But the most important agents to make rural development a success are the political and administrative will to decentralise decision making powers to the lower levels on Gandhian line with a clear policy enunciation, full political support, and needed administrative infrastructure, it is expected that the goals of real swaraj will be achieved by fulfilling the dream of the father of the Nation. It is high time for both our policy makers and the people, to turn the torch within so that they may be inspired to adopt the Gandhian way, if not for any other consideration, but for its pragmatic strength to solve our present day maladies of rural India. There is need to reiterate Gandhian values, and instead of merely garlanding the portraits of Gandhiji, India must translate his ideals into real life and make Rural India free from hunger, poverty and exploitation.

Serious steps were taken to crystallizes these ideas into concrete administrative and political structures since Independence. Recognizing the importance of democratic institutions at the grass roots level, the Article 40 of the Indian Constitution i.e., "Directive Principles of State Policy" envisages that the State shall take steps to organized village panchayats and endow them with such powers and authority as may be necessary to enable them to function as units of self-government". However, concrete steps towards decentralization of the planning process were initiated with the introduction of Panchayati Raj in Nagaur District of Rajasthan in the year 1959. The process was further intensified from the Fourth Five Year Plan (1969-74) onward. The passage of 73rd Constitutional Amendment Act however marked a significant milestone which motivated necessary changes in the instruments of Panchayati Raj acts by different States to a renewed interest in the grass roots institutions.

These developments have attracted the attention not only of administrators and political stalwarts but also of academicians and social scientists. They have probed into different dimensions of grass roots organization, the response and participation of people and the constraints experienced by them in achieving decentralized planning.

The need for decentralized planning in India has been emphasized for a long time. The large size of the country, the uneven resources endowment, the highly differentiated nature of the society in terms of language as well as institutions, the varying levels of social and economic development in different areas have made the plea for decentralized planning a weighty one. Further, competing considerations of cost of collecting data and inefficiencies in centralized planning are sought to be reconciled through introducing additional tiers of planning leading to multi-level plan process. Such multi-level plan process enables local participation, better mobilization of local resources and reduction in regional tensions. In fact, to be meaningful, planning must effectively tackle the local problems, meet the felt needs of the people and reduce even intra district imbalances. Effective plan implementation also requires plan formulation at the local level, for only those who have formulated the plans would be enthusiastic about their effective implementation. Further, it is a well-known fact that for the success of any plan, people's participation is very essential and decentralized planning provides opportunity for people's participation. Despite laudable reiterations of the Five Year Plan documents, decentralized planning with people's participation remains yet to be concretized in a multi-level planning processes in India. The inadequacy of institutional arrangements, lack of political will by shifting attitudes and perception of the policy makers to the local institutions, meagre devaluation of funds and the technocratic and bureaucratic approach to local level planning at the district level and below have come in the way of process of decentralization.

Decentralised planning is considered to be an important component of the planning mechanism in India. Till recently, planning in India has been predominantly sectoral and macro-aggregative in nature. This macro-level planning is characterized by schematic budget and special programmes. This 'top down' approach in planning gives emphasis mainly on national priorities and programmes and fails to give adequate attention to the development of area and people at the micro level. In order to correct this lop sidedness in planning in our country and also to achieve the long term plan objectives of economic growth and redistributive justice, there is a need of the balanced use of both macro and micro-level planning in the country. In other words, the predominantly centralized planning methodology which has been practiced so long in India should be supplemented by decentralized planning which ensured better perception of local needs or felt needs, better co-ordination and integration of development schemes and programmes, participation of people in all aspects of planning process at the grass-root level and better exploitation of local resources and growth potentials.

The whole idea of decentralized planning arises directly from our commitment to a democratic society, government and national political system. The purposes that decentralized planning has to serve, largely centre around ensuring: (a) that all the programmes are dynamic expressions of the felt needs of the people, every effort being made to see that it is not imputed needs which get super imposed and from the real basis of our plans and projects; (b) that there is effective participation of the local people which gives solid motivational support to the implementation of plans and leads to self-sustaining development; and (c) that above all a spirit of initiative and self-reliance is steadily built up among the people.

The present Volume, which incorporates observations of scholars from different walks of life, is based on content analysis and presents varied thoughts on the issue of decentralized planning. Of particular relevance are the observations regarding lack of peoples' participation in the multi-level planning process, inadequacies experienced in institutional arrangement, lack of political will, constraints of resources and bureaucratization of political institutions. In fact, all these factors were responsible for making decentralized planning difficult below the district level. The broad lessons that emerge from this exercise are that the institutional structures evolved from the purpose need to be strengthened, resources have to be channelled, powers have to be transferred to the local people and concomitant changes are to be brought about in administrative, political and technical arena. The policy makers, politicians, intellectuals and scientists must remember the Talisman of Mahatma Gandhi:

Whenever you are in doubt, or when the self becomes too much with you, apply the following test.

Recall the face of the poorest and the weakest man whom you may have seen, and ask yourself, if the step you contemplate is going to be of any use to him.

Will he gain anything by it?

Will it restore him to a control over his own life and destiny?

In other words, will it lead to swaraj for the hungry and spiritually starving millions ?

Then you will find your doubts and yourself melt away.

The present study is clubbed altogether in eight chapters. As usual the first chapter, i.e., introduction provides the background, review of the literature on the subject, objectives of the study, methodology and relevance of the study.

Chapter two discusses in detail the conceptual framework of planning. It also deals with the genesis, objectives and typology of planning.

Chapter three provides a detail study of the evolution of planning process in India from National Planning Committee (1937-41) to establishment of the Planning Commission. It also deals with the composition and functions of the Planning Commission and National Development Council. Apart from that, the nature of the Indian planning is also discussed in detail.

Chapter four deals with the concept of decentralized planning in detail. It also deals with the approaches to decentralized planning. It also gives a conceptual framework of decentralized planning. Finally it discusses in detail decentralized planning in India.

Chapter five gives a detailed account of the various committees and commissions appointed by Government from time to time.

Chapter six, analyses the functioning of decentralized planning in the different states.

Chapter seven deals with the future framework for decentralized planning.

In the last chapter, on the basis of research findings, some meaningful suggestions are put forward for the strengthening of decentralized planning at the gross-root level.

In the course of completion of this work, I have received immense help and co-operation from number of persons and institutions. I shall be failing in my duty if I do not acknowledge my gratitude to them.

First and foremost, my deepest gratitude to my father-in-law, Dr. S.N. Mishra, former Professor of Rural Studies, Indian Institute of Public Administration who not only introduced me in the field of Public Administration but is also a source of constant inspiration since I got in touch with him.

I have no words to express my gratitude to my wife, Dr. Sweta Mishra, Department of Political Science, Gargi College, University of Delhi, who helped me in every moment of this work and encouraged me to complete the present work within time and provided critical comments with valuable suggestions to bring this work to fruition.

I can't forget the cooperation of my daughters, Sanstuti and Sansriti, extended to me, during my research work.

I am thankful to the Librarians of the Jamia Millia Islamia, Indian Institute of Public Administration, Planning Commission, Institute of Economic Growth and Ratan Tata Library. I am also thankful to all the staff members of the Libraries for extending their co-operation whenever needed.

Last but not the least, my thanks are also due to Shri J.K. Singh for bringing out the book in a nice form and too within record time.

ANIL DUTTA MISHRA

Contents

Contents

1

Introduction

Overemphasis on block level planning in recent years is a clear acceptance of the pitfalls of centralised planning that we have been accustomed to. The basic objective behind centralised planning in our country had been to articulate national concerns and to treat micro-units as the areas where these concerns have to be implemented. However, more often than not, centralised planning tended to ignore the wide variations that exist in respect of historical experience, resource endowments, capabilities, potentials of growth, external linkage, etc., of various micro-units. As such it is not denying a reality that planned activities have generally no intimate correlationship with the felt needs of the people located in different micro-areas. Apart from this gap, the fact is that centrally planned and bureaucratically implemented development schemes do not encourage nor prefer popular decision-making and participation and do not train people in self-governance.

Therefore, the need for block level planning is a reality. However, if the planning for micro-units communities at the block level is not made by the people living in the community, it is not going to be a bit different from the old one. This is likely to be so if the values which are to be realised through planning are to be articulated by outsider, no matter however well-meaning they may be, if investigators from urban areas descend on the blocks in search of data, which are then to be processed according to a standard form in order to stimulate a predetermined pattern of output, such a procedure does not differentiate block level planning from centralised planning except for the fact that planning will be done from above but at the block level.

Side by side with the mode of planning, the most important consideration before us is planning for what? The main emphasis of centralised planning, has been to stimulate economic growth in terms of rising incomes leading to rising levels of living and reduction, if not complete elimination, of unemployment. The avowed objectives of planning in India have been not only a rapid increase in economic output but also the achievement of equality. Having these twin objectives in mind, planning in India has been geared to increasing both agricultural and individual output, improving social conditions and raising the minimum living standards of the people within a reasonably short period, and simultaneously laying down the foundation for further expansion of the economy in the more distant future.

Since the beginning of the five year plans in 1952, the emphasis has been on increasing the national income at a reasonably high rate of growth so as to secure a proportionate increase in per capita income even after making allowances for the growth in population. The idea behind such assumption has been that the increase in national and per capita incomes would progressively increase employment opportunities and the benefits of economic growth would percolate to the unemployed and poorer classes so as to improve their conditions progressively.

A crucial role has been assigned to industrialization in this strategy, which has been expected to absorb the unutilized and underutilized labour force now bottled in agriculture and the loosely organised sectors of non-agricultural pursuits and radiate stimuli throughout the economy so as to lift it out of stagnation. Directly and indirectly modern industry has been expected to raise the productivity of labour force and increase national output and income, and rising incomes are then expected to swell the volume of saving and thus finance further investment in industry. In such a vision, industrial expansion, once started, touches off a progressive spiral, leading to economy from the 'take-off' to self-governing growth. This process of industrialization is supposed to be based on capital-intensive basic industries.

The planning process is informed by world-view, even if not articulated. Since planning process and outcomes entail centralization of decision-making, concentration of power, tendency towards acquisitiveness, atomization of society, disruption of co-operative social relations and alienation, this world view and its concomitant socio-economic structure, are in many ways antagonistic to overall individual well-being. Diffusion of the world view that rests on the expectations of ever-spiralling, economic well-being made possible by defiling and plundering nature brings into operation an exploitative relationship between man, society and nature.

The block level planning has to be geared to a set of values that are different from those that are inherent in and emphasized by planning from above, if it has to avoid the pitfalls of centralized planning process. The set values must emphasize (a) dignity, well-being and autonomy of the individual in an organised social setting, (b) freedom of and opportunity for ordering individual lives in a way that enhances the changes of self-actualization, (c) participation in decision-making that affect individual life, and symbiotic harmony between man, society and nature.

Apart from the above mentioned Indian realities in regard to planning, the decentralised planning has off late become the 'sine-qua-non' to development strategy all over the world, be it the developed countries or under developed one. In our country though the attempt is being made towards decentralised planning since the introduction of 5th five year plan, yet during 80's of the century some define steps have been taken towards decentralised planning with introduction of various people oriented development schemes and creation of District Planning Board/Council all over the country.

Review of the Literature

A plethora of literature is available on planning. However, the review of the literature brings out the fact that there is not much research work done especially in the area of decentralised planning. Keeping in view the demand of decentralisation in every sphere, it is essential that planning should be decentralised and planning process should be from below not from the above or top. Despite that, this aspect of planning from below has not received much attention.

A number of books and government documents were reviewed in order to get a bird's eye view of decentralised planning in India, which was related directly and indirectly to the present study.

S.C. Nandwani's, *Planning and Development in India* (1965), throw light on some of the theoretical and current problems relating to planning and development in India and make constructive suggestions for solving them. It provides valuable insight into the nature and causes of the slow pace of economic advancement and culminates in a balanced growth-oriented study.

Y. Venugopal Reddy's, *Multi-level Planning in India* (1979), advocates multi-level planning to meet the challenges posed to the plan-process in India today—the "operation of a variety of agencies at different area levels, with different degrees of freedom with respect to defined functions". This study answers the crucial questions—such as the degree of "rationality" possible for planning in India, the regions or "area levels" that can be or are subjected to planning, the economic elements that should go into the plan process, rolling plans and their effect on multilevel planning, the possibilities of decentralised planning, and above all the reconciliation of popular participation with bureaucratic effort at all levels. The study also describes the operational and methodological problems of planning at the sub-national level, through two interesting case-studies.

P.R. Dubhashi's, *Grammar of Planning: Concepts and Applications* (1983), attempts to bring out the picture clearly about the integrated system of planning processes in simple form and it meets a long felt need and provides information on various facets of planning process in India. It also brings out the difference between principal types of planning system followed elsewhere in the world in the totalitarian and democratic plannings. Very detailed account has been given in regard to the plan formulation at the national as well as the district level, implementation machinery and monitoring and evaluation systems.

V.S. Vyas et. al., *Decentralised Planning in India* (1985), examines the experiences of decentralised planning both in government and voluntary sector. Special attention is given to planning from below. It also examines the Gujarat experience in some detail. Finally it traces the evolution of the various approaches to local level planning, and presents specific case studies. Though it is a brief work, it stimulates discussion on Planning and Decentralisation in India.

Lalitha Natraj's, *An Analysis into the Political Aspects of Planning in India: with Special Reference to Karnataka* (1985), based on extensive field-work investigates the manner in which political variables influence the planning process. Using the State of Karnataka as an illustration, she analyses the impact of federal structure, local government institutions and public participation in development planning. She has broken new grounds in linking the federal structure with that of multi-level planning. She has highlighted that state local government question is as crucial as Union-State relations question, and brought the whole picture of State level planning into a correct perspective by extending her discussion to sub-national units.

Arun Kumar Jain's, *Economic Planning in India* (1986), makes a critical appraisal of the various aspects of economic planning in India in a non-technical style and opines that most of the problems can be over-come or at least significantly reduced through better implementation, improved administration and determined political will.

Kamta Prasad in his study, *Planning at the Grass Roots* (1988), indicates the broad framework within which planning at the grass roots should be organised, discusses the reasons for its slow progress and evaluates the Indian experience with special reference to recent developments. It analyses the planning functions of institutions working at the district, block and village levels, examines the planning processes of poverty alleviation programmes like IRDP, NREP and RLEGP and provides guidelines on issues related to people's participation in the grass-roots planning. The book provides a detailed discussion of both the methodological and the organizational aspects of micro-level planning with suitable illustrations drawn from field studies. It makes meaningful suggestions for raising the quality of planning at the grass-roots, advancing several new ideas and approaches to give it a new thrust and direction.

Regional Development, Moonis Raza ed. (1988), contains thirty-one papers relating to Regional Development. The volume devotes considerable attention both to the conceptual frame within which regional development problems are analysed and to methodologies as well as techniques of analysis. An appreciation of the historical experience and an evaluation of the contemporary reality—both find their due place and sustain each other.

District Planning: A Handbook, R.P. Misra ed. (1990), centres on the theory and practice of district planning. It contains materials which constitute the foundation of the district planning process in India. The volume deals with the concepts of spatial planning, district development scheme, basic issues involved in district planning and revitalizing Panchayati Raj. Goal setting, objectives formulation and resource mobilization as well as approaches, strategies and management skill for district planning have received due attention. Apart from land and water resource analysis, agricultural production planning including that of horticulture, animal husbandry and allied activities has been looked into. Infrastructure, social services, rural employment and development administration have been studied in depth.

B.N. Yugandhar and Amitava Mukherjee's *Researches in Decentralisation* (1990), reviews the literature covering the entire gamut of multi-level planning with special reference to District Planning in India. The literature on every aspect of decentralised planning in India; regional planning in India; rationale of decentralised planning; space, spatial-organisation, region and regional organization; theories, strategies and approaches to decentralised planning, all form part of the book. Each aspect of decentralised planning has been provided with a bibliography, apart from the general bibliography and bibliographies on decentralised planning and administration; project planning; and feasibility studies and regional planning, carried out in various parts of the world.

B.N. Yugandhar and Amitava Mukherjee's, *Foundations of Decentralisation* (1990), Vol. II, explains in detail the various theoretical underpinnings of decentralised planning. The book opens with the discussion on space, regions, and regionalisation, central place theories; theories of growth pole and growth centre; theories of regional planning; growth and income generation models; principles of planning; theories of location have all been examined from a decentralised level perspectives. Even typology of planning has been dealt with in detail, to provide a clearer view of the possible character and content of planning at district and sub-district levels.

B.N. Yugandhar and Amitava Mukherjee's *Readings in Decentralised Planning* (1991), Vol. I and II, is a revised version of the papers read at the conference; the proceedings and its recommendations. The book cover everything relevant currently for district planning; the concepts, the resources, the database, the role of the administrator, the training needs, people's participation, agroclimatic zones and know-how to frame a district plan. The proceedings and the recommendations are particularly important because they are harbingers of hope and give a view of the probable shape of things as they might emerge in the foreseeable years ahead of us.

B.N. Yugandhar and Amitava Mukherjee's *Methodology and Database for Decentralised Planning* (1991), Vol. III, (consisting of three parts), first examines and then critically analyses all the major methodologies in this regard, evolved in India, starting from Gadgil's methodology down to the ones evolved by R.P. Misra and K.V. Sundaram and even Bendavid-val. It also examines the experience of the various states with regard to District Planning, particularly of West Bengal, Karnataka and Gujarat. Based on the above, a comprehensive methodology that may be adopted by various states is set forth, nothing that except for one or two notable exceptions no state in India has as yet adopted a set pattern or methodology for planning.

Sweta Mishra's, *Democratic Decentralisation in India* (1994), provides the conceptual framework of the Democratic Decentralisation. She examines in detail the process of democratic decentralisation vis-à-vis Panchayati Raj in India in historical perspectives. The real contribution is the last chapter in which future challenges to democratic decentralisation have been examined imaginatively and providing meaningful suggestions for achieving the goals of democratic decentralisation. Her study is a most significant contribution on existing literature on democratic decentralisation after passing of the 73rd amendment bill by the parliament.

The important Government documents which were reviewed were: *Report of the Team for the Study of Community Projects and National Extension Service* (1957); *Final Report of the Study Team on the Machinery of Planning, Administrative Reforms Commission* (1967); *Report of the Committee on Panchayati Raj Institutions* (1978); *Report of the Working Group on Block Level Planning* (1978); *Proceedings and Papers of the First Conference of the Heads of the State Evaluation Organisations, Programme Evaluation Organisation* (1978); *Report of the Working Group on District Planning* Vol. I and Vol. II (1984-85); *Report of the Committee to Review the Exsting Administrative Arrangements for Rural Development and Existing Administrative Arrangements for Rural Development and Poverty Alleviation Programmes* [CAARD] (1985); *Towards Improved Local Level Planning for Rural Development: Lessons from Experience* (1986); and *Report of the Commission on Centre-State Relations*, Part I and II (1988).

Objectives of the Study

In the background of introductory remarks and review of the literature, the basic objectives of the present study are as follows:

(i) To explain and examine the centralized planning and its pitfalls;

(ii) To examine and analyse the recommendations of various committees and commissions on decentralized planning;

(iii) To examine the objectives of decentralised planning as set by the Government of India based on the recommendations of the Committees;

(iv) To assess the success or failures of experiments with decentralized planning wherever it had been operative in the country; and

(v) Finally based on the analysis of the facts to provide an operational framework for maintaining effectiveness of decentralised planning.

Methodology

For the present study, we have followed the method of desk research. However, to make the study more realistic and purposeful, we have also followed the method of historical research and content analysis. The data and information have been collected basically from its published literature which are both of primary and secondary nature. The primary source consulted include reports of committees and commissions appointed from time to time and other government documents. The secondary source of data have been collected basically through the books and journals dealing with specific issue of decentralised planning. The collected data and information have been systematically analysed and presented sequenically in chapters form to make the study more fruitful and valuable.

Relevance of the Study

Though the importance of the problem is being realised since the last two decades and some studies have already appeared on the problem, however, after passing of the 73rd Constitutional Amendment Act on Panchayati Raj, decentralised planning has got added importance. As such the problem in hand has both topical and durable academic value.

2

Planning: Conceptual Framework

Introduction

Planning is the keynote, the cornerstone of modern civilization. Today, it has become quite a common practice even outside the socialist countries covering a very broad social spectrum. Planning is organised rational thought that is helpful in the determination of national objectives and in formulating policies, programmes and projects for their achievement. It has implicit relevance to institution, institution building, and institutionalization of the decision-making. Planning involves decisions on inter-sectoral priorities for making investment to achieve a desired socio-economic development of the country. This is done in the context of social values and on an assessment of the problems of the society which the planners want to solve and the needs of the society which they want to meet. Planning is necessary for achieving certain stated objectives related to a time frame and with the optimum use of resources.[1]

Planning is a process aimed at visualizing or anticipating the future situations that would emerge in the country and gear up for solving the visualized or envisaged problems. It also depicts the current problems and their magnitude and aims to solve them in predetermined time period and predetermined pace. That is, having identified the current problems the country is facing, the planning process aims to create the suitable mechanism to solve them with certain pace by allocation and efficient use of scarce sources.[2]

The pursuit curve circumscribe to achieve the prosperity is reckoned from the indicators set for achieving growth. The growth rate of the economy is one of the main objective set in the national planning. The planning for growth and economic planning for resource allocation presupposes that the benefits of the growth process are automatically subjected to redistribution through market mechanism and forces. Infact, planning is a gift of socialism. It is concerned with decision-making about investment in each sector for optimum pace of growth as well as to decide how much to invest in which sector to achieve the targeted growth. Thus planning refers to decision-making process for investment, allocation and efficient utilization of resources, economic welfare of resources, welfare, and improving the living condition of citizens of a country.[3]

Planning is of particular importance in developing countries as well as underdeveloped countries, where the government nearly always has the responsibility for the accelerated use of the available human and material resources. Long-term programmes, based on well-reasoned priorities, are invaluable for such countries, as they cannot afford to waste time, people or material. Drawing up plans, usually in the form of five-year programmes for public expenditures, in particular relating to capital formation, has in many under-developed countries become the accepted practice under which the responsible government agencies must look ahead, determine their long-range objectives and agree upon certain priorities in the light of the problem demands of the various sectors of the economy. The programme of the individual government agencies are usually coordinated by central planning office in the light of overall available financial resources.[4]

Irrespective of democratically constituted or totalitarian government it is now customary to make publicly known the intention of the government as to what they intended to do in coming few years. This can be done by two ways, i.e. either by declaring political manifesto and its implementation or by incorporating ideals and goals as constitutional guarantee and fulfilling it by creating special machinery to fulfill such constitutional guarantee. But for implementing the intention the government has to justify the priorities, expenditure and modus operandi. The development and growth has to be achieved according to well formulated, tested, and approved strategical tools.[5] The objectives of developing various sectors, say, industry, transport, power, agriculture, education, social welfare etc., to achieve specified targets need to be concretized in well-defined terms to facilitate formulation of programmes for their achievement. According to F.C. Mosher; planning involves first, the conceiving of goals and the development of alternative courses of future action to achieve the goals. Second, it involves the reduction of these alternatives from a very large number to a small number and finally to one approved course of action, the programme.[6]

The programmes and projects which are required to be implemented for achieving the national objectives need to be related to various public policies the country has adopted. This can be done by a systematic planning carried out by an apex body with the active assistance of administrative authorities, executing agencies, and other planning bodies in the country.[7]

The United Nations Publications may be cited here, which reads as follows: "The most important task facing the developing countries today is the problem of economic and social development in all its aspects. To ensure an orderly development process, it is, therefore, necessary to establish priorities, to choose rationally between realistic alternative policies and to pursue these consistently and in a coordinated manner so as to attain the short-term and long-term objectives. The concept of planning provides a logically integrated framework for taking a whole set of such decisions and the techniques of planning furnish tools for the translation of policy objectives into specific task and programmes of action. A plan then becomes a body of economic and social policies expressed in quantified targets of defined task".[8]

The planning concept ensures harmony in philosophies, ideologies and theoretical justification. It is a conscious effort to achieve desired ends in specific time. It is a rational method of application of resources for the fulfillment of specified objectives. As a systematic approach to goal achievement, planning could be undertaken by simple as well as complex organizations; by private and public sectors; at the macro and micro levels; by national and regional entities; to achieve strategic and tactical objectives.[9] Planning organises the conditions which determine and regulate economic growth. By operating the growth determinants, planning initiates the developmental process. In a strict sense, planning by itself does not bring about economic growth; it only organises the growth factors and thereby fosters and accelerates the growth process. Planning is thus only a means, a tool, and a method of action—an organised and purposive way of doing things to achieve better results.[10]

Conceptual Framework

Planning is a concept which is at the foundation of all types of organizations. It existed at all stages and ages of human civilization. Whenever rational thinking was done, planning was done. Tracing back the origin of planning to quote Mamatha Patankar it can be dated as far back as the 4th century B.C. The concept of planning is said to have been formulated by the great Greek Philosopher in his book *Republic* nearly about 2,400 years ago.[11]

Planning is necessary for systematic management of affairs, judicious and calculated use of resources aiming at making those things happen which are kept in view.

Planning is associated with various aspects. In its essence it aims to provide betterment in the living style of the people preferably to the population in lower strata. It can be defined as conscious effort on the part of any government to follow a definite pattern and route for achieving predetermined pace of economic development in order to initiate transition from one state of the traditional to new state of modernity pursue by upholding the human value without eroding the culture.[12] L. Urwick defines planning as fundamentally an intellectual process, a mental pre-disposition to do things in an orderly way, to think before acting, and to act in the light of facts rather than of guesses. It is the antitheses of gambling, the speculative tendency.[13] Planning is deciding in advance what to do, how to do, and when to do it, and where to do it. Planning bridges the gap from where we are to where we want to go. It makes possible for things to occur which would not otherwise happen. Although the exact future can seldom be predicted and factors beyond control may interfere with the best laid plans, unless there is planning, events are left to chance. Planning is an intellectually demanding process, it requires the conscious determination of courses of action and the basing of decisions on purpose, knowledge and considered estimates.[14]

Planning provides a window to peep into the future. It helps in chalking out the future course of action. Every details of the action can be worked out with the help of plan. The scope of planning is very wide as it touches each and every aspect of the future course of action. Planning is a preparation for action. It is the vital first step in any major administrative action. Planning is a means to an end. It is the process of formulating the objectives to be realized by administrative enterprise. Decisions about financial requirements, organisations, personal ends, physical facilities, supplies and equipment, work processes and many other phases of administration flow from the determination of purpose. There can be no efficient management of work performance without planning.[15]

In Public Administration, the planning process is an important part of the way in which administrative agencies participate in the political decision-making. The administrative agencies play their part in determining public policy. There is a great inter-play of political and administrative system in the country in the policy planning, which is infact the essence of an adiministrative agency with its present and future operation.[16]

L. Robbins defines "to plan is to act with purpose, to choose; and choice is the essence of economic activity". On the other hand Pt. Jawaharlal Nehru Chairman of the National Planning Committee, 1937 of Indian National Congress defines planning under a democratic society as the technical co-ordination, by disinterested experts, of consumption, production, investment, trade and income, distribution in accordance with special objectives set by bodies representative of the nation. Such planning is not only to be considered from the point of view of economics and raising of the standard of living; but must include cultural and spiritual values and human side of life.[17]

Planning pervades all aspects and forms of enterprises, whether it is private business or Government. Change and economic growth bring opportunities but they also bring risk, particularly in an era of world-wide rivalry for markets, resources and influence. It is exactly the task of planning to minimize risk which is taking advantage of opportunities.[18]

Charles R. Blitzer defined Development Planning as a complex process involving many different organisation and individual agents interacting in the formulation and execution of the country's economic and social policies.[19] A systematic planning keeping in perceptive long-range consequences is a must. Arthur Lewis lists out the following features of a development plan:

(i) A survey of current economic conditions,
(ii) A list of proposed public expenditure,
(iii) A discussion of likely developments in the private sector,
(iv) A macro-economic projection of the economy, and
(v) A review of government policies.[20]

Economic development is generally defined as increase in real per capita output or income, it is imperative that natural resources should be so harnessed in the process of production that there is optimum utilization of resources realizing in a maximum increase in national income.[21] Planning is a devise which helps in the optimum utilization of resources.

National planning can be defined as a conscious effort on the part of the government to create conditions for the maximum utilization of the resources—both human and material for engendering and directing development. In India, the Five Year Plans are the instrument for changing the social and economic structure of the country.[22]

Planning for economic development implies external direction or regulation of economic activity by the planning authority which is, in most cases identified with the

Government of the State.[23] Gadgil considers that planning is not a once for all effort, it has to be a continuous, consistent and forward-looking effort, sustained for decades. Planning effort is an organizational effort undertaken systematically by an external authority. Planning is aimed for all round progress and economic planning is only one aspect of planning. There are other aspects of planning which influence economic planning. In this respect, the First Five Year Plan Report had observed that economic development depended upon a variety of factors which constitute the psychological and sociological sitting within which the economy operated.[24]

Planning today is supposed to be the panacea for all economic ills. The modern government has become the agent to use the instrument of planning for improving the socio-economic conditions of the people. Planning means conscious and coordinated efforts organised by the States. When state interference expands and covers the whole of national economy with certain predetermined objectives, it is called economic planning.[25]

Economic planning essentially works out a rational solution of economic problems by coordinating means and ends. A planned economy functions under a great measure of control over economic resources and varying degrees of state intervention and is concerned with creating adequate institutional framework, policies and measures which would uplift the lot of the people. It is through planning that various processes of social and economic changes can be initiated.[26]

Planning is an instrument of socio-economic development of the people. Modern states are welfare states and the administration is development oriented. Planning for the nation is for the all round development of the people.

Planning, therefore it follows, is essentially a way of organizing and utilising resources to maximise advantages in term of defined following elements: *(i)* the visualisation of a clearly defined goal to be achieved and the path, system to be followed, *(ii)* exploration of available resources, physical and other, which virtually condition the former and, *(iii)* their full exploitation and optimum allocation, in terms of concrete programme of action, spread over a period of time, in different spheres.[27]

Genesis of Planning

Planning for economic development is entirely a gift of Marxism to mankind. There has, of course, been development without a plan and plans for the achievement of some partial or limited objectives which do not directly owe anything to Marxism. But a total plan for sustained and balanced economic growth was for the first time embryonically conceived by Marx and Engels, and the first country to actually undertake such a venture was the Soviet Union.[28] In other words, Soviet Union was the pioneer country to apply the principles of planning, as a component part of its State policy, to task of economic reconstruction.

The Marxian concept of planning is, in fact, organically linked up with its analysis of capitalist social relations on the one hand and the dynamics of a socialist society, which is to replace the former, on the other.[29]

This is not to belittle the historical role of capitalism in economic development, to which Marx and Engels paid their unstinted tribute: "The bourgeoisie, during its rule of scare one hundred years, has created more massive and more colossal productive forces than have all preceding generations together. Subjection of Nature's forces to man, machinery, application of chemistry to industry and agriculture, steam navigation, railways, electric telegraphs, clearing of whole continents for cultivation, canalization of rivers, whole populations conjured out of the ground—what earlier century had even a presentiment that such productive forces slumbered in the lay of social labour?"[30]

But in all this, there was neither any concrete action, nor any clear pre-vision of ultimate outcome of the totality of actions undertaken by innumerable separate entities. As Maurice Dobb puts it, "the decisions affecting development", in a capitalist economy "are in the hands of autonomous entrepreneurs, or firms motivated by considerations of individual profit...in such an economy development does not occur as the result of any thought-out and co-ordinated plan. It just happens—accidentally as it were—as the result of a large number of autonomous individual decisions, each of them taken in ignorance, of other and parallel decisions, on the basis of market data plus guess-work or 'expectations' as to the future movements in that market data. In such circumstances the horizon of each decision taker is straitly limited both in space and over time.[31] At times "Dobb elaborates on another occasion", these expectations, spread to become a general market 'mood' which evokes something like unanimity of action among all and sundry. In this way an investment boom may develop, during which investment in new productive capacity outruns demand under capitalist conditions; however, such booms are wont to be short-lived and to collapse as soon as any wide-spread conditions of excess capacity becomes apparent.[32]

Development under capitalism, however imposing over the historical span, was never an uninterrupted spiral, but all through marked by booms and slumps. The dynamics of its growth was very piquantly depicted by Engels as early as in 1877. "As a matter of fact, since 1825, when the first general crises broke out, the whole industrial and commercial world, production and exchange among all civilized peoples and their more or less barbaric hangers on, are thrown out of joint about once every ten years. Commerce is at a standstill, the markets are glutted, products, accumulate, as multitudinous as they are unsalable, hard cash disappear, credit vanishes, factories are closed, the mass of the workers are in want of the means of subsistence, because they have produced too much of the means of subsistence; bankruptcy follows upon bankruptcy, execution upon execution. The stagnation lasts for years; productive forces and products are wasted and destroyed wholesale, until the accumulated mass of commodities finally filter off, more or less depreciated in value, until production and exchange gradually begin to move again. Little by little the pace quickens. It becomes a trot. The industrial trot breaks into a canter, the canter in turn grows into the headlong gallop of a perfect steeplechase of industry, commercial credit, and speculation, which finally, after break-neck leaps, ends where it began—in the ditch of a crisis. And so over and over again. We have now, since the year 1825, gone through this five times, and at the present moment (1877) we are going through it for the sixth time".[33]

The crisis, which end 'in a violent explosion', are as Marx

and Engels so brilliantly analysed, caused by the 'contradiction between socialised production and capitalist appropriation', inherent in the capitalist system.[34] Although periodic crisis consistently dogged its step for over a century since capitalism came of age, the growth of the productive forces on balance showed remarkable uptrend till World War First. It was only in the post-War I era, and more particularly after the crisis of 1929, that the full impact of the critical forces generated within the world capitalist system affected this basic trend and production level was pushed well below that of 1913.[35] It was the impact of the great crisis that led to serious heart-searchings among the more objective minded leaders of the capitalist world, some of whom arrived at the conclusions 'startling' for themselves, that 'something was fundamentally wrong' in their system. For example, Lloyd George said in a speech at Cambridge in April, 1933: "If we had not had a great war, if we had gone on as we were going, I am sure that sooner or later we would have been confronted with something approximately like the present chaos. There must be something fundamentally wrong with our economic system, because abundance produces scarcity."[36]

With this background the protagonists of the capitalist system undertook a critical study of its working so as to locate its weak points and devise measures as how best to strengthen them. This led to the flowering up of new schools of western economic thought, which sought to introduce certain element of partial, if superficial, planning within the basic framework of capitalism[37].

There is an important, qualitative difference between planning in socialist and capitalist economies. In the former, planning is the means for rapid, sustained and balanced economic, social and cultural growth; in the latter, it is not growth but solution of certain problems created by growth itself; in another words, it constitutes the method to correct, remedy or prevent certain unwanted developments which are inherent in the capitalist economy itself.[38]

Planning as has been stated earlier, was first embryonically conceived by Marx and Engels as the antithesis of anarchy inherent in capitalism. As early as in 1948, in the first mature document of the emerging new social philosophy, i.e. the manifesto of the Communist Party, they made a broad formulation of the main tasks which later came to be designated by the general term 'planning'. The German term *planwirtschaft* (meaning Planned Economy) could be treated as appropriate term to signify origin of the concept of planning[39].

It is well known that it was the Soviet Communists who first translated the dream of a planned society into reality. As well as early as 1903 the Bolsheviks had adopted in their programme substitution of "... the social ownership of the means of production and exchange for private ownership" and the introduction of "the planned organisation of the social production process in order to ensure the well-being and all-sided development of all the members of the society". After 1917 revolution the implementation of five years plans changed the face of that country within a considerably short period. Soviet Government set up in December 1917, the Supreme Council of National Economy under its direct control. The council was entrusted with the task of regulating and co-ordinating the economic life of the country. Along with the progress of nationalization of industry and transport, its functions also continued to be enlarged. The new regulations governing the Supreme Council, adopted in August 1918, authorized this body besides the task of organising and regulating production and distribution to directly manage all the State enterprises as well.[40]

The next step in planning was the GOSPLAN (State Planning Body), constituted in 1921, which was commissioned by the USSR Government in 1927 for drafting of plans, and consequently the First Five Year Plan was put into action in 1929. Since then the economic structure of that country has always been governed by plans.

Attracted by the spectacular achievements of planning in USSR, some countries tried to introduce planning, in their countries, for regulating the economy. Nazi and Fascist economies were built around planned efforts. The 'New Deal' of USA was also a plan for recovery of the economy from the shadow of depression of 1930. Now almost all the countries of the world have launched their plan for development.

Chronology of Plan

Modern economics, particularly development economics, national accounts system, commitment to socialism tenets etc. makes planning as scaffolding on which growth and welfare struggle is continued. Planning is un-American but pro Russian. Infact, planning process is a unique gift of Soviet Union was established in 1925 and its first five year plan came into existence in 1928. Other plan dates are as follows:[41]

Germany	1933 first Nazi four year plan.
Italy	1933 Vanoni Plan.
U.S.A.	1933 development of Tennesse Valley in USA.
Turkish	1934
India	1951 after independence first five year plan.
Ghana	1951 when British colony its first plan.
	1957 Second and Third Plan of Ghana.

In 1964 about 125 nations had development plan. Out of 125 nations about 93 were termed as developed countries in 1964. In Western Europe among the democracies United Kingdom was first nation to have overall plan after World War II. Other countries to follow U.K. were Netherlands, Norway, France, Sweden and Denmark.

India is seen, by world communities in general and developing countries in particular, with great curiosity for her development, governance and struggle for amelioration of poverty. India after her independence in 1947 had opted for transformation of agrarian, traditional and dead economy on the path of industrialization and modernization. In consonant with prevailing thinking of 1950s, India has also created a agency called Planning Commission in March, 1950.

Objective of Planning

We have seen that planning is a scheme of action covering entire structure of the economy, an attempt to pool together the available resources of the country and direct them in a manner that will realise the defined social and economic goal. In industrially advanced countries the emphasis is given on correction of short-comings of the economic system and ensuring of more equitable distribution of benefits. As the problem is of underemployed equipment and resources and under utilization of labour in the form of unemployment the planning may be aimed at increasing the "aggregate demand with a view to stimulating the economy to full employment".

In underdeveloped countries the difficulty is that of "insufficient equipment and utilizable resources and under utilised labour" therefore the problem is that of increasing the rate of capital formulation—capital equipment and utilizable resources. According to Dr. V.K.R.V. Rao "the process of economic development is essentially one of increasing productivity or output with a view to raising the national income, standard of living and economic welfare, for which the measures required are:—

(i) increasing value of utilizable resources,

(ii) increasing value of capital equipment,

(iii) increasing value of efficiency of labour,

(iv) increasing value of state of knowledge, and

(v) increasing incentive for maximising output."

The planning may aim at the achievement of the following objectives:—

1. Full Employment;
2. Equality of Incomes;
3. Lower Prices;
4. Maximum Production; and
5. Increase in National Income or Raising of standard of living.[42]

These objectives are, though interrelated, competitive in nature and all of them can not be realised simultaneously. There is, therefore, the problem of choice, balancing of these competitive objectives—the problem of balancing, selecting is the core of all economic problems.

Now it is universally recognized that the ultimate goal of all economic policy should be the achievement of full employment. Unemployment is the most serious economic and social problem of modern society. There are difficulties in the way of accepting full employment as immediate objective of planning. The programme of employment can only be implemented after the structural deficiencies in the economy have been ratified. Because firstly, the policy of increasing employment without corresponding increase in production will force the prices upward and, secondly, the expansion of employment opportunities to absorb the growing population will impel sacrificing indefinitely the feuits of technological advancements, as such a measure involves a matter of time and immediate solution can only be sought through small scale production. Hence the policy of Full Employment can be pursued effectively only after the economy has gained a certain momentum.[43]

Economic equality and social justice are conditions indispensable for the survival of democracy. A carefully worked out policy for reduction of disparities in income and wealth is the sine-qua-non of planning. Only increase in national income and wealth can not raise the level of general living, but an equitable distribution of benefits accruing to the society as well as a result of development plans to raise the per capita income and ultimately the standard of living, is essential.[44]

Underdeveloped economies are characterised by inflationary trends or rising prices. This is partly due to growing demand without proportionate increase in the value of production and partly due to the deliberate attempt of individuals, by unfair hoarding of available stocks. Inflationary trends should be kept under control, by price control, rationing, state-trading etc. methods, so that it may not assume spiral form. However, slightly rising prices greases the wheels of economic progress during initial stage.[45]

The present condition of underdeveloped economies warrant a rapid increase in the output of essential consumption goods. But large and early increase in the consumption and a high rate of capital formation, which involves curtailment of consumption, can not go hand in hand. The sub-normal standard of living and marginal income limits the scope for saving and investment. Thus there is a problem of reconciliating these two conflicting ends. To some extent this may be compromised by mobilizing the idle resources of the community.[46]

The ultimate aim of planning is the increase in National income on which the standard of living of the community depends. In the initial period there is a problem of choice between immediate increase in the standard of living by producing more essential consumption goods on one hand, and capital formulation for future and stable growth of the economy by concentrating on producers and capital goods on the other. The later is the better choice. Effort should be made in the direction of diverting a major part of additional income accruing for development purposes. Increase in the national income is the devise of economic progress.[47]

Thus the plan has to be drawn up "in terms of a scheme of priorities as between these objectives", laying more stress on some and less on other considering time and circumstances prevailing in the country.

Elements and Step in Planning

A clearly well defined ultimate goal, the attainment of which should be the governing force behind the entire national activities, economic, social, political, must glitter before the eyes of the nation. The vision of such a distant panoramic dream, bestowing the ray of hope, inspires people to greater activity, endeavor, industry and co-ordination, which can ultimately help in transforming static factors into dynamic forces. Most of the underdeveloped countries have either no such defined, clearly perceived goal set before them or the knowledge about the model of a pattern of society—capitalistic, socialistic etc.—to be built. The result is the manifestation of ideological bankruptcy, social chaos, disorder, confusion, and un-coordination and mal-adjustment of economic, social and political activities. The planning efforts must be directed towards a mutually accepted goal. The five factors namely the Economic Forces, Financial Resources, Political Set Up, Psychological Forces and Administrative Efficiency are essential for the success of planning.[48] The elements of the planning includes:—

1. type of institutions,

2. accessibility of education,
3. channel of information,
4. commitment to Social and Economic Welfare,
5. monitoring macro aggregates,
6. financial and capital market and evolution of institutional arrangement,
7. monitoring externalities, immobilities, monopolies, economics of scale, fiscal and financial matters,
8. role of public sector and private sector.[49]

The formulation of planning involves number of steps. First step is assessment of resources, including financial aspect, and way of increasing the same: A complete survey of physical and other aspect and collection, compilation and classification of available statistics are necessary. Second is fixation of priorities: after obtaining full knowledge of economic condition and natural resources. Priorities should be fixed in the light of the ultimate objective and should aim at balanced and sustained utilization of existing resources. The priorities may be *(a)* agricultural development with emphasis on reformation of modus operandi and attainment of self sufficiency in food—the top most problem, *(b)* construction of power projects; for providing cheap power, *(c)* expansion of essential goods industries, and *(d)* establishment of heavy and basic industries and development of capital and producers good industries.

Third is factors retarding progress must be find out and steps be taken to counteract them by suitable measures, and setting up of suitable machinery at various levels and stages for implementing the plan.

Fourth is determination of target. After the exploratory moves, the physical targets are to be fixed for each industry, towards the attainment of which the planning efforts are directed during the given period. The following points are the guiding factors in fixing the target:—

(a) it should not be vague and be expressed in figures,

(b) it should not be based on balancing of priorities and be determined in relative sense rather than in absolute sense,

(*c*) it should correspond to the available resources, or should not be over-ambitious or underestimated,

(*d*) it should have co-relation between production and utilization of resources, and

(*e*) it should be flexible, open to necessary correction at a later period, if needed.

Fifth is appraisal or review of progress should be made from time to time. The common lists or method of checking the progress are the increased efficiency, allocation of optimum factors of production, increase in the volume of production, creation of external economics and statistical surveys.

Further, a good plan should posses the following characteristics. Firstly, it should possess flexibility and must not be wedded to rigid dogmas. Modifications and alteration in the light of the experiences gained, changed requirements and circumstances must be made from time to time. Secondly, it should cover the entire sector of economic life, aim at developing economic as well as social, political, educational etc. spheres and avoid lopsided building of economic sector only. Thirdly, it must aim at balanced utilization of unexploited resources, and have long term as well as short term policy with a view to solve temporary as well as permanent disequilibrium. Fourthly, it should contain certain programmes for parallel maintenance of private sector—the economic institutions in the beginning are predominantly under private sector—at least during first few phases of planning, in conformity with the overall plan, and sphere of operation of private and public sector should be demarcated to avoid wasteful competitions. They should be complementary to each other.[50]

Typology of Planning

Within a broad classification of centralised and decentralised planning process there could be substantial diversity. The multi-dimensional phenomenon in economy, region and space is germane to articulation of the development process along different bases. Typology of planning is conceived from different perspectives. Thus, there could be comprehensive planning or partial planning; indicative planning or imperative planning; planning by compulsion or planning by inducement; totalitarian planning or democratic planning; sectoral planning and spatial planning; physical planning or financial planning; perspective planning or long range planning, short range planning or annual planning.

Comprehensive or Partial Planning

Comprehensive planning connotes planning for the totality of the economy. It takes into account the aggregate resources available within the economy and aggregate targets to be reached by the economy as a whole. In socialistic economics where all except the most minor means of production are socially owned, planning of necessity has to be comprehensive.[51] On the other hand partial planning signifies planning for a part of the economy. Partial planning partakes the nature of planning for a particular element in the economy, like public investments, and its consequence on the economy as a whole is left to be taken note of in national accounting and statistical analysis. In fact the distinction between comprehensive planning and partial planning, is a difference based on the substance and scope of planning.

Imperative Planning and Indicative Planning

Indicative planning is a system in which the plan lays down the general framework of goals and targets whose fulfillment is left to the various participating economic institutions. Imperative planning, on the other hand, is a system in which the fulfillment of plans is not left to the spontaneous efforts of the participating economic agencies and institutions, but is brought about through various instruments of control and devices of regulation imposed by the state.[52] The distinction between imperative planning and indicative planning is related to the methodology of planning. The fact remains that indicative planning admits of greater flexibility and more individual initiative of agencies and institutions of change, than in case of imperative planning. The concept of indicative planning is noted in the theory of demand expectations (and in the planning techniques adopted in French and other West European plan models) which enjoins that the "rate of growth that can be achieved is, within limits, partly a matter of the growth rates that the relevant bodies in society (particularly entrepreneurs) expect to be achieved."[53] The distinction is explained by W. Arthur Lewis[54] as follows:

"The distinction between an 'indicative' and 'controlling' plan is important. The (imperative) plans made by communist countries are documents of authorization; they tell each industrial unit what it must produce and how much it may invest. A Development Plan (of an indicative type), on the other hand, authorises nothing. Even public expenditure is authorized not by the plan but only by the Annual Budget passed by parliament."

Variation in the content of the degree of freedom allowed for individual action and initiative, in imperative planning and indicative planning, explains the genesis of the appellations "planning by compulsions" and "planning by inducements" applied to these two planning types respectively. The distinction between these two planning is based on the techniques deployed in ensuring achievement of targets. Thus, planning by compulsion would include a whole battery of physical controls like allocation of raw materials and intermediate products to various production unit in industry and agriculture, rationing of consumer goods, quotas of foreign exchange, permits and licenses for setting up industries, etc. Planning, by inducement, on the other hand, is a system in which there is a resort to various fiscal and monetary devices by the planning or central governmental authorities—devices like taxations and subsidies, manipulation of prices and tariffs, rates of interests including the bank rate, open market operations, floation of loans and debentures etc. An economist has described planning by compulsion as planning by biting and planning by inducement as planning by barking.[55]

Totalitarian Planning and Democratic Planning

In totalitarian planning, the Leviathan lives and breathes to impose an all pervading discipline: workers, managers, consumers, farmers and indeed all people in the field and in the factory, at home and on the roads, in offices and in chambers, are left with little choice, if at all and are called upon to walk along the well beaten path. Democratic planning seeks to embody people's aspiration into the plan, and is based on formulation and implementation of plans on the basis of people's will and preferences.[56] In other words, planning and democracy are inherently incompatible with each other. In fact, Prof. Hayek has described planning as a road to serfdom, Prof. Schumpeter has also pointed out this as a major danger in socialism. All powers of economic decision-making would be concentrated in the hands of planners; gradually but inevitably this would mean that all important decisions not only in economic but in other fields would tend to be concentrated in the hands of the ruling authorities. Planning would thus inevitably degenerate into bureaucratic tyranny. Indeed, democracy as a political system cannot survive too long in an economic system managed through comprehensive totalitarian planning. On the other hand, it is argued that planning and democracy far from being incompatible with each other are indeed complementary. Plans would succeed only to the extent they evoke voluntary support of the people and only democracy can inspire popular support to planning. To quote Barbara Wootten: "It is the detail of planning and detailed execution of the plans that the ordinary citizen has most of real value to contribute". The tyranny of planning, she suggests, could be effectively avoided if "every incursion of government into economic planning is accompanied by creation of small local organs of citizens to co-operate in the execution of centralised plans. The last and greatest defence freedom under planning lies in the quality and attitude of the people... It is the citizens of a well planned society who are least likely themselves to fall victim to the dangers of planning and vice versa".[57]

Centralised Planning and Decentralised Planning

The planning process can be differentiated between centralised and decentralised planning, based on territorial levels where they are sought to be operationalised. In centralised planning the entire plan is conceived, implemented and monitored from a central location, for the country as a whole, and despite existence of a hierarchy of economic planning regions and administrative delineation. In a decentralised planning framework, on the contrary, planning at several levels for the relative level of economic planning region or administrative boundary, is conceived, executed and evaluated. Centralised and decentralised planning are often referred to as "single level" or "multi-level" planning, and the appellations reveal the character and concept involved in these planning phenomena.[58]

Macro-level Planning and Micro-level Planning

Macro-level planning means planning at the national level. Micro level planning means planning at division, zone, state or group of states level. Micro-level planning operate at district or block level. On the other hand, local-level planning is planning at the block, village level or cluster of settlements level. These variants are planning essentially by territorial space size in descending order of magnitude.

Usually a national plan encompasses all the sectoral plans and integrates them into a comprehensive whole to typify a macro-plan. There may be, however, production and resource planning for any individual producing unit, say a district, which partakes the nature of micro planning. Such micro-level planning does not mean much when viewed from the national perspective unless the different micro-plans of the different inter-related areas, are well co-ordinated which is possible only against the backdrop of national economic planning or at least, micro-level planning.[59]

Short-term, Medium-term and Long-term Planning

If time element is injected in differentiating types of planning, there could be three types of planning, depending on the time profile: the short-term planning, medium term planning and the long-term planning. The short-term plans are directed to tackle situations requiring only small scale variations in production and employment pursuits as against long-term planning that deals with institutional and structural changes for long-term socio-economic development. In other words a short-term plan could be a plan spanning over a year or two, and a long run plan could be in respect of ten or fifteen years. A medium range planning, is an intermediary concept between short run and long run planning say a plan covering five year or so.

Physical Planning and Financial Planning

In physical planning, the factors of production, namely, land, labour, capital, raw materials etc. available within the economy is taken account of during the process and period of planning. Financial planning relates to planning of financial resources, emanating from various sources like taxation, borrowing, deficit financing, foreign aid, public debt and the entire spectrum of sources. The availability of these resources have to be matched against the demands of the physical plan. The essence of financing planning is to ensure that demands and supplies are matched in a manner which exploits physical potentialities as fully as possible without major and unplanned changes in the price structure...the outlay is fixed in terms of money and the estimates are made on the basis of various hypothesis regarding the growth of national income consumption, imports etc., to cover this outlay by taxation, savings and the increase in cash holdings. The financial part of the planning is concerned with the financial provisions for carrying out the physical programmes of the plans. In that perspective, physical planning and financial planning complement each other, and must be carried out concurrently, each in harmony with the other, for the success of a play, for whatever level and dimension it may relate to.

Sectoral Planning and Spatial Planning

Planning appertaining to the various sectors of the economy, each as a constituent unit of the macro plan for the economy as a whole, is called sectoral planning. On the other hand spatial planning is planning for development i.e., development plans for each homogeneous unit into which the country may be demarcated, on the basis of "physio-cultural" space reality. Spatial planning is particularly suited for attempts at geographic dispersal of efforts and manifests itself in the formation of spatial sub-systems and regions. Integrated development of resources, social justice founded on fair dispersal of plan activity and advantages of optimum location, embodied in spatial planning efforts, provide validation for adoption of spatial planning for development with justice. Whereas in sectoral planning, development as evident in space is the consequence of sectoral plans, in spatial planning, sectoral developments emanate from an integrated spatial plan.[60]

Adaptive or Developmental Planning

Spatial planning could be either "adaptive" or developmental. Adaptive planning depends upon a recognition of the influence of the general pattern of development on the spatial system. Development planning is conceived of as a response to the pressures and requirements of national economic development. The task of adaptive planning is then to streamline the process of spatial evolution so as to achieve at any point in time on spatial structure which matches the needs of industry for efficiency and growth. Developmental planning on the other hand sets itself a more ambitious task. Based on the recognition of the interplay and feedback relations between economic development and spatial evolution, it seeks to identify and achieve within a dynamic and historical context a pattern of evolution of the spatial structure that at any point of time is judged to be the most efficient from the point of view of promoting a sustained process of rapid economic development. In this way, the spatial organization of the economic and socio-cultural activities is conceived as a means to promote long term development.[61]

Economic and Developmental Planning

To define planning from the point of view of programme content, led to the classification of planning as economic planning and developmental planning. Economic planning, prima facie, is more fashionable in developed economies, where social capital and infrastructure essential for the required quantitative expansion and structured adjustment of the economy already exists. Development planning is more suited for developing countries, where the necessary social capital and infrastructural facilities are inadequate or non-existent to start and sustain economic development. But its very nature, development planning is experimental and differ quite demonstrably from economic planning both in its imperative and indicative variants, in so far as development planning involves both economic and social factors as elements to be planned as against only economic factors incorporated in a purely economic planning exercise. Development planning, involving policy intervention and action programmes, attempts at accomplishing economic, social and institutional reforms together with economic growth. In a broader sense, development planning means planning for human transformation, a task which is much more arduous, much more intriguing and at once, comprehensive than that of accelerating growth in a growing economy—the task of economic planning. It is likely, therefore, that is formulating and implementing development plans, objectives and techniques may have, often, to be subjugated to social policy.[62]

Normative or System Planning

The planning process, whether sectoral or spatial, whether economic or development can partake the nature of either normative or systems. As the word indicates, normative planning enjoins upon planners a search for the best possible results with regard to the goal set, clearly enough the emphasis has to be on a low key in relation to social and institutional dimensions of planning. The normative approach to planning takes in reckoning five groups of problems—

1. the procedure for defining goals and objectives;
2. the phasing of the plan as also defining of sequences and linkages;
3. inter-linking and integrating sectoral and functional elements of the plan;
4. inter-linking and integrating territorial plans, and finally
5. determining the contribution that specialists can put into the system and co-ordination of the specialists activities.[63]

Physical planning provides a classical example of normative approach, where the planner is converted into an expert, an analyst, a surveyor, a model maker and an operator all moulded in one, quite unconcerned, about what would be the fate of the plan, were the environment, in which the planner operates, to undergo change and transformation, or even turn hostile. The planners role is limited to the mere formulation of the plan for the best possible results in relation to the established goal, leaving the implementation part to the executive embodied in the politicians and to the elements that make the politico-administrative structure of the economy. The plan, designed to achieve best results for the established goals, in a dynamic world is bereft of flexibilities which are essential to make it meaningfully operational.[64]

The systems approach to planning in contrast deems the exercise of planning as a social process operating in a highly stochastic word and in the context of a varying and varied socio-technical content. The planning system is conceived of as a structure, formed by constituent elements of values, goals, roles, factors of production, organization and their clientele, rules, norms, regulations and the enter-relationship between individual and collective participants of planning. The elements of a systems approach to planning could be as under:[65]

- *(i)* Values, ideologies and goals;
- *(ii)* Execution of the developmental task; task to be undertaken by planning;
- *(iii)* Organizational framework by which the development tasks are to be executed;
- *(iv)* The executives, specialists and professionals participating in planning; and
- *(v)* The accepted norms and set rules that regulate the inter-relationship between individual participants and individual organizational units and roles of the executors.

Rural, Urban and General Planning

Rural, urban and general planning classification is based on environmental phenomenon. Rural planning is concerned with planning for rural areas. A plan that relates to rural development is a rural plan. Urban plan similarly relates to plan for the urban areas. The plan that encompasses both a rural and an urban territory without having regard to either its urban or rural bias, is the general plan. An urban or a rural plan seems to have more operational significance when the regionalisation of the economy is directed to demarcate the territory as urban or rural.

Fresh-End and Diagnostic Planning

This classification of planning is based on availability of investment resources. If planning has to be resorted to, like that of geonomic space, a new start with adequate finances, be made which one could call Fresh-End Planning. It is akin to zero-based budgeting in budgetary exercises where the new budget is prepared on a clean state without having any regard for the past budget. In contrast, if within the structure of long standing spatial organization of the society, planning is to be adopted, given that resources are limited, it would be what is known as diagnostic planning.

Typology of Planning at Local Level

The pressure of international and domestic circumstances that affect local needs in the process of local economic development, and the realization that intra-national local economics are affected differently, that is, some have growing economy while others are experiencing stagnation, are the two conditions that affect local economic development. There are two economic development perspectives: responsiveness to external needs or responsiveness to local domestic needs. While the external needs characterizes much of the prevailing practice, local responsiveness is identified with a new, emerging (or latent) practice, which has set the stage for proposing a typology of four distinct planning orientations: two prevailing models (contingency planning and strategic planning) and two emerging models (contingency planning and strategic planning) for local economic development that are growing or declining. These four approaches has been called preactive, reactive, practice and interactive approaches respectively to planning.

Recruitment Planning

Recruitment planning is the traditional approach to economic development used in many sub-national economies, to attract firms and industries, where public involvement is limited. Private sector vitality and initiative tend to displace expressions of local concern for explicit planning, to operate on the assumption that all business is good for the local economy. Industrialisation of the area is taken for granted as an obvious policy, which is generally linked with a tacit understanding that industrialisation will benefit the entire community. Planning based on this approach includes a wide range of industrial inducements and efforts to enhance the image of the territorial tier's "business climate". Because it is the most familiar style of local economic development planning, variants of recruitment planning can be found in nearly every locality in the developed countries, particularly the United States. Recruitment planning represents a typical preactive approach to external conditions, that is, the local economy is initiating action to build or preserve its economic super-structure as a response to competitive conditions.[67]

Impact Planning

Impact planning is of relatively recent origin, which focuses attention on efforts to mitigate or reduce the worst effects of industrial losses in a local economy, and is grounded on the concern for the effects of lock out, particularly the impacts on the labour force, and is episodic in nature. This activity constitutes the most recognizable public sector planning approach to economic development, an approach based heavily on the continued availability of funds from higher levels of governments. The main assumption underlying this approach, is that action is taken only at the time of crisis, which does not admit of flexibility in response and over-emphasizes the obtention of external funds. In backward areas, firms close down or gradually reduce operations of older, less profitable plants, which is a strategy that is basically the mirror image of the industrial growth cycle for growing areas.

Development activities are implicit in the term impact planning, and typically a programme is brought on by sudden, unexpected lock out and similar employment activity cutting down actual and potential employment opportunities. Development policies and planning in this approach have an orientation of dealing with the local impacts of necessary, but uncontrollable, acts of industry. And as Blackly rightly points out the "programmes associated with such policies are generally targeted on, or other strategy is subordinate to, the real long-term needs" of the area.[68] Clearly enough the planners wait till the circumstances change adversely. Impact planning is thus reactive planning in reaction to loss of existing industrial base.[69]

Contingency Planning

Contingency planning grows out of the ineffectiveness of impact planning in declining areas, and from an awareness that planning must anticipate future course of events and not react to them once they actually catch on the local economy. Impact planning by its conceptualization responds to episodes of economic distress only after they have afflicted the economy and therefore, actions taken does not really fit into an overall plan for the micro-level economy. Moreover, efforts to mitigate these impacts are primarily devised to reduce the effects of relocation of firms and industries. Contingency planning is carried out in areas susceptible to economic distress, and therefore, contingency planning must take account of future dislocations from external forces which are stochastic in nature and which cannot be predicted or controlled at micro-region level. Contingency planning can help mobilize an area's resources and inherent capabilities to deflect or accommodate impacts brought on by external forces. The process of contingency planning enjoins the assessment of the strength of all economic sectors and anticipates prospects for industrial dislocation, plans potential economic redevelopment projects, and provides community organizations and leaders with the information necessary to initiate actions at the sub-national regional level or at micro-planning level. For these tasks to be effectively presented, contingency planning will probably be conducted by a local economic development organisation and development department.

In contingency planning, policies towards industry, labour, and enterprises at the local level would reflect the felt needs of the people. As a matter of fact, contingency planning, as a distinct form of planning, emerged only after efforts initiated by the people demonstrated a clear need for it, and was established as a device for weaker sections of the populace to exercise economic power in otherwise strong local economics. Thus contingency planning is an interactive approach which recognises the need to be flexible to conditions as they emerge, and as a consequence it is more thoughtful and takes account of the totality of the local, regional and national economic conditions.[70]

Strategic Planning

Strategic planning is the most appropriate approach for all micro-level planning, and it is a future—oriented planning approach that builds the economy of the place on the basis of people's felt needs perspective. It is "utilization of all [locality's] forces, through large scale, long-range planning and development to ensure (success)". Strategic planning entails large-scale efforts to deploy available resources, which implies that economic development is considered as an objective for all ongoing local community governance functions, and that regulations, tax policies, public works, and local government programme expenditures be framed with a long term view of economic development, where economic development specialists are put at the focal points of budgeting, public procurement, expenditure patterns, and finance, all requiring a form of local economic planning. A distinguishing feature of strategic planning is that selection of projects are based on people's needs and resources and not on the opportunities that present themselves as we go along, which implicitly enjoins that all actions are subject to local decision making favouring no particular form of industry.[71]

Different typologies of planning distinguished above arise out of different ways of looking at the system of planned economy. A planned economy combines within it different concepts of planning connected with each other. Thus, comprehensive, imperative, totalitarian, physical planning based on compulsory directions tend to go together and are characteristic of centralised planning in socialistic economy. Similarly, fiscal measures are characteristic of planning in market-oriented western economics. However, these should not be considered entirely exclusive of each other.

REFERENCES

1. K.L. Handa, "Planning and Budgeting in India: Concept and Practice", *Indian Journal of Public Administration,* Vol. XXX, No. 3, July-September 1984, p. 660.
2. Ratnakar Gedam, *Development Planning: Origin and Growth,* Akashdeep Publishing House, New Delhi, 1991, p. 2.
3. *Ibid.*, p. 3.
4. UN, *A Handbook of Public Administration,* New York, 1961, p. 93.
5. Ratnakar Gedam, *op. cit.*, p. 3.
6. Frederick C. Mosher, *Programme Budgeting,* Public Administration Service, Chicago, 1954, pp. 48-49.
7. K.L. Handa, *op. cit.*, p. 662.
8. United Nations, *Government Budgeting and Economic Planning in Developing Countries,* New York, 1966, p. 3.
9. M.J.K. Thavaraj, "Politics of Planning", *Indian Journal of Public Administration,* Vol. XXX, No. 3, July-September 1984, p. 515.
10. K.N. Bhattacharya, *Indian Plans A Generalist Approach,* Asia Publishing House, New Delhi, 1963, p. 12.
11. Mamatha Patankar, *Economic Planning,* Sultan Chand and Sons, New Delhi, 1977, p. 138.
12. Ratnakar Gedam, *op. cit.*, p. 22.
13. L. Urwick, *The Elements of Administration,* Harpur and Brothers, New York, 1943, p. 33.
14. Harold Koontz and Cyril O'Donnell, *Essentials of Management,* Tata McGraw Hill, New Delhi, 1980, p. 55.
15. F. Morstein Marx, *Elements of Public Administration,* Prentice Hall of India, New Delhi, 1968, p. 113.
16. *Ibid.*, pp. 114-115.
17. Birendra Kumar, *An Introduction to Planning in India,* Bookland Private Ltd., Calcutta, 1962, p. 2.
18. F. Morstein Marx, *op. cit.*, p. 56.
19. Charles R. Blitzer, *Economy wise Models and Development Planning,* Oxford University Press, London, 1977, p. 1.
20. Arthur W. Lewis, *Development Planning: The Essentials of Economic Policy,* George Allen and Unwin Ltd., London, 1966,

p. 13.

21. Ruddar Datt and K.P.M. Sundaram, *Indian Economy*, S. Chand and Co., New Delhi, 1973, p. 133.
22. Mary Parmar, *Development Planning in India*, Reliance Publishing House, New Delhi, 1992, p. 3.
23. D.R. Gadgil, *Planning and Economic Policy in India*, Asia Publishing House, Poona, 1965, pp. 150-151.
24. Mary Parmar, *op. cit*., p. 4.
25. B.C. Tandon, *Economic Planning: Theory and Practice*, Chaitanya Publishing House, Allahabad, 1970, p. 4.
26. Mary Parmar, *op. cit*., p. 4.
27. Birendra Kumar, *op. cit*., p. 2.
28. Ajit Roy, *Planning in India: Achievements and Problems*, National Publishers, Calcutta, 1965, p. 1.
29. *Ibid*.
30. Karl Marx and F. Engels, *Manifesto of the Communist Party, Moscow*, 1953, pp. 53-54.
31. Maurice Dobb, *Some Aspects of Economic Development*, University of Delhi, Delhi, 1951, p. 11.
32. Maurice, Dobb, *Economic Theories of Growth, etc*., Enquiry, P.P.H., Delhi, p. 1.
33. F. Engels, *Anti-Duhring*, Moscow, 1954, pp. 381-382.
34. Ajit Roy, *op. cit*., p. 3.
35. *Ibid*., p. 5.
36. *Ibid*.
37. *Ibid*., pp. 6-7.
38. *Ibid*., pp. 9-10.
39. Ratnakar Gedam, *op. cit*., p. 1.
40. Ajit Roy, *op. cit*., p. 16.
41. Ratnakar Gedam, *op. cit*., p. 27-28.
42. Birendra Kumar, *op. cit*., pp. 10-15.
43. *Ibid*., pp. 16-18.
44. *Ibid*., p. 18.
45. *Ibid*., p. 19.
46. *Ibid*., pp. 19-20.
47. *Ibid*., pp. 20-21.
48. *Ibid*., pp. 21-22.
49. Ratnakar Gedam, *op. cit*., p. 44.

50. Birendra Kumar, *op. cit.*, pp. 29-30.
51. P.R. Dubhashi, *Grammer of Planning: Concepts and Application*, IIPA, New Delhi, 1983, p. 19.
52. *Ibid.*, p. 20.
53. B.N. Yugandhar and Amitava Mukherjee, *Foundations of Decentralisation*, Heritage Publishers, New Delhi, 1990, p. 37.
54. W. Arthur Lewis, *Development Planning—The Essentials of Economic Policy*, George Allen and Unwin, London, 1960.
55. P.R. Dubhashi, *op. cit.*, p. 22.
56. B.N. Yugandhar and Amitava Mukherjee, *op. cit.*, p. 38.
57. P.R. Dubhashi, *op. cit.*, pp. 23-24.
58. B.N. Yugandhar and Amitava Mukherjee, *op. cit.*, p. 39.
59. *Ibid.*
60. *Ibid.*, pp. 41-42.
61. *Ibid.*, pp. 42-43.
62. *Ibid.*, p. 43.
63. *Ibid.*, pp. 43-44.
64. *Ibid.*, p. 44.
65. *Ibid.*
66. *Ibid.*, p. 45.
67. *Ibid.*, p. 46.
68. Edward Blackley, *Planning Economic Development Theory and Practice*, Sage Publications, Newbury Park, 1989, p. 83.
69. B.N. Yugandhar and Amitava Mukherjee, *op. cit.*, p. 46.
70. B.N. Yugandhar and Amitava Mukherjee, *op. cit.*, pp. 47-48.
71. *Ibid.*, pp. 48-49.

3

Planning in India: Historical Background

Introduction

India is listed among the Third World countries. The Third World with 70 per cent of total population, subsists on only 20 per cent of the world income and even this meager income is so mal-distributed internally as to leave the bulk of its population in abject poverty.[1] The third world countries are characterised by low level of living, poor quality of human resources, high rate of population growth, unemployment and disguised unemployment, dependence on the primary sector of the economy, i.e., agriculture and agriculture based industries, low capital formulation, etc. Thus these countries share a common goal, i.e., reduction of poverty, inequality and unemployment, provision of minimum level of education, health, housing and food to every citizen.[2]

To achieve these goals, planning has become essential. In fact, in any social system planning has become the major instrument to achieve the social and economic goals. Planning is essential for development. Development and planning go hand in hand. There can be no development without proper planning. India's experimentation in democratic planning on such a vast magnitude to reconstruct, rebuild a new India, the entire structure of national life, is perhaps first of its kind in the history of mankind.

Historical Background

From early times, the movement for political advance in India was linked up closely with social and economic development. Leading public men like Dadabhai Naoroji, M.G. Ranade, R.C. Dutt wrote extensively and social and economic problems. Their main themes were the poverty of the people and the recurrence of famines, which they attributed to the defective land-revenue policies of the government, the high cost of administration and deficits in the balance of payments. They were convinced that no solution could be found for the economic backwardness of India by British Governments pledged to a policy of laissez-faire and non-interference in social matter. It was their view that only national Government which would actively promote economic development by direct governmental action could bring about improvement in living standards. The resolutions of Indian National Congress from 1929 onwards emphasized the need 'to make revolutionary changes in the present economic structure of society and to remove grave inequalities in order to remove poverty and ameliorate the condition of the masses.'[3]

The National Planning Committee (1937-41)

The Government of India Act of 1935 introduced provincial autonomy. This led to the formation of Congress Governments in eight provinces. Soon after this, in August 1937, the Congress Working Committee passed a resolution suggesting that an inter-provincial committee of experts should be set up to consider 'urgent and vital problems, the solution of which is necessary to any scheme of national reconstruction and planning' and 'to suggest how and in what order those should be tackled'. This was followed later in the year by the constitution of the National Planning Committee of which Shri Jawaharlal Nehru became the chairman.[4] This was the first practical attempt to draw up a co-ordinated plan for national economic regeneration in 1938. This committee was the outcome of the conference held in July, 1938 which felt that the problems of poverty and unemployment, of national defence and economic regeneration could not be solved without rapid industrialisation.[5]

The committee consisted of 15 members including well-known industrialists, economists, financiers, professors and scientists; and in addition representatives of the Provincial Governments (the non-Congress Provincial Governments of Bengal, Punjab and Sind also co-operated) and those of the Indian States of Hyderabad, Mysore, Baroda, Travancore and Bhopal. It was a remarkably representative committee cutting across political boundaries as well as the high barrier between official and non-official India, except for the fact that the Government of India was not represented.[6]

The principal objective of planning was to attain, as far as possible, national self-sufficiency. The fundamental aim was to give to the masses a basic irreducible minimum of human existence.

The committee appointed 29 sub-committees to study and report on different sectors of the economy. However, the work of the committee was interrupted due to the outbreak of the World War II and the imprisonment of its members. The sub-committee carried on this work in spite of various impediments and submitted report on their respective fields—some in 1939 and 1940 while some in 1945 and 1946. This appreciable work of the committee generated great interest and discussions in the problems of national planning.[7]

The Bombay Plan (1944)

Another systematic effort towards evolving a national plan for the country was made in 1944 in the form of "A Plan for Economic Development in India" by eight leading businessmen of the country,[8] popularly known as the Bombay Plan. The plan envisaged an outlay of Rs. 10,000 crores, spread over a period of 15 years, the principal objective being to bring about a doubling of the per capita income by tripling the national income. The outlay was divided among different sectors.

The plan devoted thought to problems connected with state control and state ownership. It also recognized that during the planning period controls might have to be instituted similar 'to those which are in force at present under war conditions'. Dealing with methods of state intervention the plan defined the respective fields of ownership, control and management of economic enterprises by the state of the three factors, the plan considered state control to be more important than ownership or management from the point of view of maximum social welfare. It contemplated a wide field for state control which might assume the following forms: fixation of prices, limitation of dividends, licensing, auditing, prescribing conditions of work and wages of labour, etc. The plan also defined the fields considered desirable for state ownership. In its view state ownership had a place in two classes of causes: '*(i)* where the state finances an enterprise which is important to public welfare and security; and *(ii)* where the state ownership is a necessary means of enforcing state control'. As for the planning organisation, it proposed that there should be a National Planning Committee, representing different interests to prepare a detailed plan and that execution should be the responsibility of a supreme economic council under the Central Government. Details of the relationship of those bodies with provincial and regional Governments were not worked out. Finally, the plan described the general shape of the economic organisation which would emerge if the proposals were carried out—"it will be not unlike the type of society which Prof. A.C. Pigon foreshadows in his book *Socialism vs. Capitalism*".[9]

In fact, the publication of Bombay Plan resulted in initiating and stimulating lively discussions on economic planning in the country. A number of other private plans viz., "The Peoples Plan", "The Gandhian Plan", and "Sir M. Visvesvaraya Plan" followed the Bombay Plan.[10] As these plans were more or less based on varying objectives and different approaches, their significance for the country at large was limited.

People's Plan

The 'People's Plan', promoted by M.N. Roy of Radical Democratic Party and the Indian Federation of Labour in reply of Bombay Plan. The plan envisaged satisfaction of basic needs, cloth, food, shelter, with 10 years at a expected cost of Rs. 15,000 crores. Lured by the spectacular achievements of Russian and German plans, People's Plan advocated nationalisation of Agriculture and liquidation of rural indebtedness on finances, it was even more utopian than the 'Bombay Plan', for it believed that with the extension of public ownership to industry and collective ownership to agriculture, development could become 'self-financing' within six years. It also proposed a control of private industry and commerce, during the 'transitional' period, so rigorous that complete stultification could have been the only result.[11]

Gandhian Plan

The Gandhian plan was drawn by S.N. Agarwala in his book "The Gandhian Plan". The central point of emphasis was very different from all the other plans. Its inspiration was Gandhi's view of life which no other plan reflected—not even the N.P.C. report. Agarwala derived his position on economic development from Gandhi's economic thought which, in a sense, controverts the first axim of economics, viz., that wants are unlimited and illimitable. This is reflected in the following quotation from Dr. J.C. Kumarappa, an ardent follower of Gandhi: "There are wants which are primary needs and there are also wants which are artificially created".[12] Agarwala talked of the need to preserve human values in a rapidly decaying world of little or no sense of values. The village would, therefore, be the pivotal point of development. This was justified by India's unemployment problem and because it was in line with the Gandhian ideal of simplicity. Moreover, it would have none of the exploitative violence of industrialisation. Agarwala quoted Gandhi: "Pandit Nehru wants industrialisation because he thinks that, if it is socialised, it would be free from the evils of capitalism. My own view is that the evils of capitalism are inherent in industrialisation and no amount of socialism can eradicate them".[13]

Commenting on the Gandhian Plan, A.H. Hauson writes: "Essentially, this was no plan at all, but an essay in economic morality, preaching the virtues of simplicity, manual labour, local self-sufficiency, decentralisation, and independent village community. Where strictly economic arguments were used, they merely provided additional support for proposals based on moral principles."[14] In his plan, Mr. Agarwal put a case for use of natural as distinct from artificial fertilisers and for location of key industries in villages. This plan revealed the impossibility of reducing Mahatma Gandhi's scattered and sometimes ambiguous dicta in economic organisation to a logical and coherent system. Yet it was not without a more positive importance. In its popular emphasis on popular participation and its insistence that the willing co-operation of the ordinary villager must be won, it anticipated panchayati raj. Also of value was its attempt—however unrealistic—to define the objectives of planning in terms of a way of life, as well as in terms of percentage increase—in per capita income. Gandhian plan also advocated four-fold increase in standard of living and in per capita income respectively in 10 years.

Table 3.1 Outlays in the Plans

Plans	*NPC*	*Bombay*	*Govt.*	*People's*	*Gandhian*
Targets	Double standard of living	Triple National Income		Four times standard of living	Four times per capita Income
Time period	10 years	15 years	5 years	10 years	10 years
Total outlay (in Rs. millions)		1,00,000	12,950	1,50,000	35,000

Source: A Kundu, *Statistical Measures of Effects of the Five Year Plans in India,* Thesis submitted to London University, 1959.

Post-war Reconstruction—The Government of India (1941-46)

The Government of India took up the consideration of plans of post-war reconstruction in June 1941, when a committee was appointed under the Member of the Executive Council in charge of commerce. Later, a Reconstruction Committee of the cabinet was set up with the viceroy as chairman and members of the Executive Council, as members. The committee has a secretariat under it, with a number of panels of experts. In June 1944, the Government of India created a Planning and Development department under a separate Member of the Executive Council for organizing the planning work in the country and co-ordinating it. To assist the department, there was a Planning and Development Board consisting mainly of Secretaries of economic departments. The departments of Central Government, Provinces and Indian States were invited to prepare detailed plans. More than 20 panels were set up consisting of officials and technical experts for plans of industrial development. For the plans of Central Ministries, Provinces and State Governments, the total financial resources, Central and Provincial, estimated to be available were of the order of Rs. 1200 crores. Most of the panels set up submitted their reports. When planning had advanced and sufficient experience had been gained, the Government of India found it necessary to explain to the country what their industrial policy was. Accordingly, on 26th April, 1945, they issued their 'Statement of Government's Industrial Policy'. This is an important pronouncement, as the last one to be made by Government responsible to the Secretary of State for India and marks a complete departure, as a result of the lessons of the war, from policies hitherto followed.[15]

In 1946 the work of planning had been practically completed and the Planning and Development Department was abolished.[16]

Advisory Planning Board (1946)

In October 1946, the Government of India appointed a Committee called the 'Advisory Planning Board' with the following terms of reference: '*(a)* to review the planning that has already been done by the Government, the work of the National Planning Committee and other plans and proposals for planning; *(b)* to make recommendations in the light of this review for the co-ordination and improvement of planning; *(c)* to make recommendations as regards objectives and priorities, and *(d)* to make recommendations regarding the future machinery of planning'. At that time the Government of India was composed of the Viceroy and an Executive Council of Indian leaders (under the Cabinet Mission's scheme). The Congress leaders joined the

Government in September and those of the Muslim League in October 1946. The two groups held widely divergent views on basic issues. Obviously without a knowledge of the nature of the future constitution, the Advisory Board could make no far-reaching proposals.[17]

The Board recognized the need for central planning and control for the development of large-scale industries. As regards the future planning organization, the Board recommended the setting up of a 'single, compact organisation which would be responsible to the cabinet (or to a committee of the cabinet)' for *(i)* scrutiny and co-ordination of States plan; *(ii)* formulating plans for development of major industries and important minerals; and *(iii)* making recommendations for state aid to and control of industry, monetary and financial policy, trade both internal and foreign, etc. This body should also watch implementation and publish reports. As regards the form of organisation, the following recommendation was made: 'This organisation, we think, would best take the form of a small wholetime Planning Commission composed of not more than five and not less than three members and furnished with all the necessary secretariat facilities and with appropriate technical assistance...'.

As regards the composition of the Planning Commission, it has been suggested that the chairman should be a senior minister, holding no portfolio, like the Lord President of the Council in England. Some of us think that such an arrangement has much to commend it, but are doubtful whether in view of existing political conditions in India it would be practicable; while other think that it is better in any case to dissociate the commission entirely from the vicissitudes of politics. 'We recommend, therefore, that no minister should be a member of the Planning Commission and that it should be, as far as possible, a non-political body whose members will not fluctuate with changes in political fortunes'...'We suggest that if the commission consists of five members, as some of us recommend, it should be composed as follows:

(i) A person of standing with general experience of public affairs, who would be the chairman.

(ii) Two non-officials with knowledge and experience of industry, agriculture and/or labour.

(iii) A Government official with knowledge and experience of finance and general administration.

(iv) A person eminent in the field of science and technology.[18]

A Consultative Body of 25 to 30 members was also recommended which would meet half-yearly (or quarterly, if necessary). This would consist of the members of the Planning Commission, representatives of Provinces and Indian States and representatives of different interests—agriculture, industry and commerce, labour, etc. This Body will advice or problem and receive progress reports.

The report was published in January 1947 'to elicit constructive criticism from a considerable body, of opinion in the country'.

However, the plans put forward except those of the National Planning Committee suffered from limitations. The Government of India of 1941-46 knew that their tenure was to be short-lived and that transfer of power was bound to take place quite soon. The work of the Advisory Planning Board had also to be conducted under similar limitations. The plans were not co-ordinated. They embodied recommendations made by technical experts without consultation with State Governments or other interests concerned and they had no social philosophy behind them. With the advent of Independence, the plans became inadequate, though the thinking on the techniques was useful for the future.[19]

From Independence to the Establishment of the Planning Commission (1947-50)

The constituent Assembly recognized that there should be fundamental changes in the social structure. India should become a welfare state, the general pattern of which was to be set out in the constitution. The welfare state should not only promote social and economic development on a much larger scale than hitherto envisaged with the widest measures of social justice possible, but should also presence and strengthen the traditional values based on human dignity and peace and tolerance. In April 1948, the Government of India issued a resolution on Industrial Policy. It defines the immediate objective of national policy in these terms: 'The nation has now set itself to establish a social order where justice and equality of opportunity shall be secured to all the people. The immediate objective is to provide educational facilities and health services on a much wider scale, and to promote a rapid rise in the standard of living of the people by exploiting the latent resources of the country, increasing production and offering opportunities to all for employment in the service of the community. For this purpose, careful planning and integrated effort over the whole field of national activity are necessary; and the Government of India propose to establish a National Planning Commission to formulate programmes of development and to secure their execution'.[20]

The most important step taken by the Government of India was the appointment of the Fiscal Commission in April 1949. It was to recommend the future policy to be adopted in regard to protection and assistances to industries and the machinery to implement such policy. The Commission submitted its report in April 1950. On the basis of the pattern of society envisaged in the constitution, the Commission made proposals for co-ordinated and balanced development of all sectors of the economy. 'Rationalization of agriculture and industrial advancement' are in reality parts of a single programme.[21]

The constitution was enacted on 26 November 1949. It came into force on 26 January 1950 and the establishment of the Planning Commission on 15 March, 1950 followed as a logical sequence. The newly established Planning Commission was called upon to formulate programmes of development on the socialistic principles. Further, the National Development Council was set up in August, 1952 to strengthen and mobilise the efforts and resources of the nation in support of the Five Year Plans and to promote economic policies in all vital spheres and to ensure the balanced and rapid development of all parts of the country. The Planning Commission works in accordance to the broad guidelines indicated by the National Development Council.

The Planning Commission

After Independence and with the integration of former Indian States with the rest of the country and the emergence of new geographical and economic order, a fresh assessment of the financial and other resources and of the essential conditions of progress became necessary. The need for comprehensive planning based on a careful appraisal of resources and factors became imperative. It was felt that these purposes could best be achieved through an organisation free from the burden of the day to day administration but in constant touch with the Government at the highest policy level. Accordingly, the then Finance Minister in his Budget speech on the 28th February, 1950 announced the Government's decision to set up a Planning Commission with the passing of the Cabinet Resolution of 15th March, 1950 the Planning Commission was constituted. The only major departure from the recommendations of the Advisory Planning Board is in respect of the character and status of the Planning Commission, which is much high-powered and more political body than one envisaged by the Board.

Functions

The following were the task assigned to the Planning Commission vide Government of India Cabinet Resolution dated 15th March, 1950:

(i) make an assessment of the material, capital and human resource of the country, including technical personnel and investigate the possibilities of augmenting such of these resources as are found to be deficient in relation to the nation's requirements;

(ii) formulate a plan for the most effective and balanced utilization of the country's resources;

(iii) on a determination of priorities define the stages in which the plan should be carried out and propose the allocation of resources for due completion of each stage;

(iv) indicate the factors which are tending to retard economic development, and determine the conditions which, in view of the current social and political

situation, should be established for the successful execution of the plan;

(v) determine the nature of the machinery which will be necessary for securing the successful implementation of each stage of the plan in all its aspects;

(vi) appraise from time to time the progress achieved in the execution of each stage of the plan and recommend for adjustments of policy and measures that such appraisal may show to be necessary; and

(vii) make such interim or ancillary recommendations as appear to it to be appropriate either for facilitating the discharge of the duties assigned to it; or, on a consideration of the prevailing economic conditions, current policies, measures and development programmes; or on an examination of such specific problems as may be referred to it for advice by Central or State Governments.

Besides the above functions, the Government of India (Allocation of Business) Rules have assigned responsibilities to the Planning Commission in respect of—

(a) Public cooperation in national development,

(b) Hill area development programme,

(c) Perspective Planning, and

(d) Directorate of manpower.[22]

Composition

The Prime Minister of India has been from the beginning the Chairman of the Planning Commission and has participated in and given direction to the thinking on all major issues of policy. The Commission has a Deputy Chairman and a number of full time members.[23] The Minister for Planning is usually the Deputy Chairman of the Planning Commission. The members include political and non political persons. From the political side, the Union Ministers holding charge of important subjects like finance, industry, energy, agriculture, human resources, law and justice are members of the Planning Commission. The non-political persons are usually eminent persons from social and technical fields.[24]

The Planning Commission has a number of Advisers who perform a very important role. The Advisers help the commission in keeping close touch with progress of planning and its implementation in states. Each Adviser (State Plan) has a group of States/UTs. These Advisers tour the states from time to time and are an active link between the Planning Commission and the State Governments. These Advisers also head the various divisions of the Planning Commission. At present the work of the Commission is organised in 27 Divisions. They are headed by Advisers/Joint Secretaries/ Joint Advisers. All the Divisions in the Planning Commission may be grouped into three types of divisions vis-à-vis; Administration Divisions, General Division and subject Divisions.[25]

National Development Council

The National Development Council was set up in August, 1952 on the suggestions of the Planning Commission and is regarded as the most significant step for promoting understanding and consultation between the Union and State Governments on planning and common economic policies.[26]

The main objective of the National Development Council was to strengthen and mobilise the efforts and resources of the nation in support of the plans to promote common economic policies in all vital spheres and to secure the balanced and rapid development of all parts of the country. The claim for popular democratic sanction behind the plan rests on the ground that this body comprises mainly of the elected representatives of the people at large as well as on the ground that a wide scope is given for public discussion on the plan in its draft form.[27]

Initially, the NDC was composed of the Prime Minister of India, the Chief Ministers of all states and, the members of the Planning Commission. On the recommendations of the Administrative Reforms Commission, the council was reconstituted and now composes of the Prime Minister, all Union Cabinet Ministers, Chief Ministers of all States and Union Territories and the members of the Planning Commission. The Cabinet Resolution redefined the function of NDC on 7th October 1967 are as follows:

(i) to prescribe guidelines for the formulation of the national plan, including the assessment of resources for the plan;

(ii) to consider the national plan as formulated by the Planning Commission;

(iii) to consider important questions of social and economic policy affecting national development;

(iv) to review the working of the plan from time to time and to recommend such measures as are necessary for achieving the aims and targets set out in the national plan, including measures to secure the active participation and cooperation of the people, improve the efficiency of the administrative service, ensure the fullest development of the less advanced regions and sections of the community and, through sacrifice borne equally by all citizens, build up resources for national development.

Nature of the Indian Planning

Planning in India is neither capitalist nor communist. As we know by this time, there is no national planning in the capitalist countries with macro-economic projections, output targets or priorities in the investment programme. Individual firms of course make their own plans to increase their productivity efficiency. But this cannot be considered planning in the conventional sense in which it in used. In India, there is a conscious effort on the part of the Government to create conditions for engendering and directing development. The Five Year Plans embody the policies and programmes of the Government for changing the social and economic structure of the country. These plans form a continuing series, both in terms of investment and in benefit. The first Plan was set against a simple projection of economic growth over a period of thirty years from 1951 to 1981. The second plan was worked out in relation to a perspective upto 1976. The third plan was drawn up as the first phase of a fifteen year plan for the period 1961-76. The projections of the fourth plan are presented upto 1980-81, so that detailed investment planning in the

Fifth Plan (1974-75 to 1978-79) will take fully into account the need for advance preparation in respect of additional output in long gestation sectors to be realised in the early years of the sixth plan. This shows that plans in India present a picture of continuity. Of course there are important changes from one phase to another, in output targets, in investment priorities, in social and economic policies and in programmes of economic activity, reflecting both changing conditions and problems and the results of fresh experience and evolution. But planning at the macro-level continues as a regular process, an indication of fundamental differences between India and the advanced capitalist countries.[28]

On the other hand, the socialist goals of the Indian economy alongwith macro-economic planning delude many people to think that India is going the communist way. The goals and methodology may look alike, but the operational mechanism is very much different. There is a world of difference between the goals of communist countries and those of India. The point we need to emphasise here that the Indian Plan is dissimilar to that of the former Soviet Union since India is not prepared to accept the totalitarian and monolithic state, it does not want a planned economy with state monopoly of international trade and finance and with complete nationalisation of the means of production. In fact, planning of a command type as prevalent in former Soviet Russia and other Communist Countries can not be possible in India where eighty-five to ninety per cent of production is done in enterprises over which the Government has no direct control.[29] The important features of Indian planning is as follows.

Democratic Planning

Indian planning is essentially democratic in character. It aims to enlist not only the support of the masses but also their active participation in plan preparation and implementation. It is generally held to mean that this popular participation and co-operation should emerge voluntarily, so that state policies can be carried out without regimentation or coercion. As stated is the First Plan, "Public co-operation and public opinion constitute the principal force and sanction behind planning. A democracy working for social ends has to base itself on the willing assent of the people and not the coercive powers of the state... In this way any programme is conceived, offered and carried out, action by the agencies of the government must be inspired by an understanding of the role of the people and supported by practical steps to enlist their enthusiastic participation". This only implies that India has a deep attachment to the values of freedom. That is why each plan has been developed by a prolonged process of consultation and public debate, so much so that planning in India has emerged as a feature of national consensus largely passing beyond party lines.[30]

Decentralisation in Planning

Indian planning is not so comprehensive even though aggregate targets are fixed in each plan. The greater part of the plan refers to programmes of development undertaken by the Central and State Governments. These include a variety of measures, some involving direct enterprise and management, some in the nature of extension and promotion and others providing for training, research and other methods of raising productivity. The private sector which constitutes a major part of the economy is not planned in detail. Plan in this sector are in nature of estimates and forecasts undertaken in consultation with the representatives of industry, but sufficient provision is made for financial resources, including foreign exchange, and the requisite material resources to facilitate the execution of these plans. The levels of production aimed at are also in the nature of estimates, although they serve as target guides.[31] The five year plans in India do not have also force of legal enactment. The plans do not automatically come into force; special legislation has to be undertaken in the context of specific objects to attain the desired change. The Planning Commission which is entrusted with the responsibility of drawing up the plans in the country is just an advisory body. The resolution of the cabinet which specified the duties of the Planning Commission also indicated the Commission's role in the system of Government: "The Planning Commission will make recommendations to the cabinet. In framing its recommendations, the commission will act in close understanding and consultation with the ministries of Central Government and the Governments of the States. The responsibility of taking and implementing decisions will rest with the Central and the State Governments". This shows that the Planning Commission does not have any legal authority, nor have its power, responsibilities and terms of reference changed during the period of its existence.[32]

In regard to State Plans, the Commission does not have much authority. In view of the fact that India has a Federal Government and the subject of economic and social planning is in the "Concurrent" list, the power of the Planning Commission has been confined to only supervisory and guidance work. In fact, the States make their own plans for submission both to the Planning Commission and to their own legislatures. The final plan of each State is inevitable the product of a compromise between State and Centre, worked out through discussion with Commission; but it is the State's own planning handiwork that provides the basis for discussion. Further, even though each States has a planning machinery to prepare plans, there is no uniformity in the pattern or procedure of plan-making in the States. This means that planning in India has made possible a degree of interpenetration of interest and concern between the Central and State Governments.[33]

Socialism in India

Socialism has been accepted in India as a long-term strategy for economic advancement. The term 'Socialist Pattern of Society' which was elaborated in the Second Five Year Plan and quoted both in the Third Plan and Fourth Plan clearly indicates that economic policy and institutional changes have to be planned in a manner that would secure economic advance along democratic and egalitarian lines. The positive goals of socialism imply the raising of living standards, the enlargement of opportunities for all, the promotion of enterprise among the disadvantaged classes and the creation of a sense of partnership among all sections of community.[34] Prime Minister Nehru who was the main architect of Indian socialism explaining the concept once said "... we have accepted only the broad principles of socialism not the dogma and orthodoxy of socialism in its rigidity. And if necessary we can revise even principles which we have accepted".[35] And this principle according to him is a system of economic organisation in which everybody has a rising standard of living, where power is not concentrated and so on and so forth.[36]

Noted economist Gunnar Myrdal analysing the concept and practice of socialism in India has observed, "Indian socialism is an ideology propagated by an intellectual elite, who are convinced that socialism is desirable on rational grounds as a means for development and for achieving greater equality".[37]

All this means that Indian socialism implies the following concepts:

(a) Planning the resources of India for economic development and increase in employment opportunities with a view to increasing the standard of living of the people;
(b) Equitable distribution of income, so that the relatively less privileged classes of society can increase their economic and social status;
(c) Progressive reduction of concentration of incomes, wealth, and economic power for establishing a just social order;
(d) Democratic process of change to create a sense of involvement among all sections of the community in the transformation of society; and
(e) Expansion of the public sector with a view to strengthening the control of the Government over the commanding heights of the economy.[38]

In fact, the broad objectives of socialism is rapid economic development by continuous progress towards equality and social justice.

Relation between Private and Public Sector

Though the importance of the public sector has been emphasized in Indian Planning, it does not belittle the importance of the private sector. First of all, the socialist ideology of state ownership and management are contemplated only for a limited number of fields; public utilities, large-scale industry, mines, large plantations, banking, insurance and to some extent, commerce, agriculture, with the exception of large plantations. Small-scale industry and crafts are not regarded as a potential targets for socialization. In case of agriculture, decentralisation, ownership and management is favoured. In the case of small-scale industry and crafts, co-operation is relied upon to combine the benefits of decentralisation and of economics of scale. It is stated in the Second Plan, "our socialist pattern of society implies the creation of large numbers of decentralised units both in agriculture and industry. These small units can obtain the advantages of scale and organisation mainly by coming together". This shows that there is no attempt in India to establish a monolithic type of organisation. In fact, the Industrial Policy of 1956 clearly recognised the need for the private sector. It divided industries into three categories. The first category consisted of 17 major industries whose future development will be exclusive responsibility of the State. These industries refer to such strategic and basic industries like arms and ammunitions, atomic energy, iron and steel, heavy machinery, etc. Further, the Industrial Policy Statement contains no threat of nationalisation to the existing units included in the first category and operating in the private sector. The second category contains a list of 12 industries which will be progressively State-owned and in which the State will therefore generally take the initiative in establishing new undertakings, but in which private enterprise will also be expected to supplement the efforts of the State. These industries are fertiliser, machine tools, antibiotics etc. The second category of industries distinctly emphasises the need for co-operation between the private and the public sector. In the third category, there is a list of residual industries whose future development will be left to the initiative and enterprise of the private sector, though it will be open to the State to start any industry even in this category. However, it will be the policy of the State to facilitate and encourage the development of these industries in the private sector, in accordance with the programmes formulated in the successive Five Year Plans, by ensuring the development of transport, power and other services and by appropriate fiscal and other measures. The Industrial Policy Statement therefore clearly envisages a mixed economy. In an economy which is wedded to a socialistic pattern of society, it is very necessary that the industrial undertakings in the private sector should necessarily fit into the framework of the social and economic policy of the State and be subject to the control of and regulation by the State. In fact, the purpose of expanding the public sector in big industries is mainly to influence the speed and direction of economic development.[39]

In a poor country with a large and rapid growing population, industrialisation has a strategic role both for absorbing the surplus population from land and for improving the technological base of the economy to increase production, employment and income in the country. In fact, industrialisation is the key to modernisation. It is therefore thought that the industrial sector in a country will set the pattern for economic development. It may therefore be said that the enlargement of the public sector, as envisaged in the planned programme of the country, has little to do with an ideological choice between socialism and free enterprise. It is more concerned with social justice and economic growth.

Operational Control

Though India relies heavily on physical or direct controls, it does little physical planning in a substantive sense. The plans are not constructed on the basis of detailed calculation of input requirements and output expectations of physical factors, goods, and services in the various sectors of the economy. On the other hand, it has become customary in India to prepare a fiscal plan in the context of an overall savings and investment exercise. Since Indian plans are based on western theories and models, which have to do with savings, investment and output, the plan is presented in terms of financial aggregates. Therefore, the structure of Indian plans are financial or more narrowly fiscal in character with bits and pieces of physical planning. While Indian plans are fiscal plans, focusing attention on public expenditure, and in particular, public investment, there is a whole system of operational controls over the private sector which are discretionary in nature. These discretionary operational controls are tools of short-term policy imposed with a view to controlling the activity of the private sector and directing economic activity on the basis of plan objectives. A financial plan is however expected to rely more on non-discretionary controls. In fact, in Indian plans, preference has been given to non-discretionary operational control like the use of price mechanism as a means of implementing the plan. For example, it is stated in the Draft outline of the First Five Year Plan. "For the fulfillment of the objectives defined in the plan, it is necessary to have a price policy which secures an allocation of resources in conformity with these objectives. In the private sector, decisions are made in the light of prevailing prices and expectations as to their future trend. Unless the alignment of prices favours the use of resources along the lines indicated by the targets worked out for this sector, there is likelihood of a serious discrepancy between the results expected and the actual achievements. A change in price relationships in one line has its repercussion on the distribution of resources in several other lines. In the absence, therefore, of an effective policy aimed at maintaining an appropriate structure of prices, planning in respect of the private sector can not succeed".[40]

But in practice, administrative discretionary control[41] have become the standard procedure, indeed the very essence of planning in India.[42] It is of course maintained that as planning becomes more comprehensive and its scope increases, indirect methods and controls (that is non-discretionary controls) will gain in preponderance.[43] However, the present situation is very different. These discretionary controls alongwith socialism lead many people to remark that India has a centralised plan. There are mainly two reasons why these negative discretionary controls have become preponderant in India. One is that of economic necessity. Since the economic system in India is not sufficiently integrated and the non-discretionary controls are relatively ineffective, there is reliance on discretionary controls. The second force working in this direction is the vested interest of administrators and politicians. These controls invest power in administrative officials and politicians to grant licences, to overlook violations of regulations and to show favour to particular industrialists and business-men. These controls therefore add greatly to the incentives for the rewards for graft and corruption. Once the administrative machinery is improved, probably there will be less need for negative discretionary controls.[44]

REFERENCES

1. V.M. Sinha, *Personal Administration: Concept and Comparative Perspective,* R.B.S.A. Publishers, Jaipur, 1986, p. 28.
2. D. Ravindra Prasad, et. al. comp., *Administrative Thinkers,* Sterling, New Delhi, 1989, p. 47.
3. V.T. Krishnamachari, *Fundamentals of Planning in India,* Orient Longmans, Bombay, 1962, p. 31.
4. *Ibid.,* pp. 31-32.
5. B.C. Tandon, *Economic Planning in India,* Chaitanya Publishing House, Allahabad, 1975, p. 419.
6. V.T. Krishnamachari, *op. cit.,* p. 32.
7. Kewal Panjabi, *The Civil Servant in India,* Bharatiya Vidya Bhavan, Bombay, 1965, p. 341.
8. G.D. Birla, J.R.D. Tata, Sir Purshotam Das Thakurdas, Shri Ardeshir Dalal, Sir Shriram, Kasturbhai Lalbhai, A.D. Shroff and Dr. John Mathai.
9. V.T. Krishnamachari, *op cit.,* pp. 35-36.
10. C.N. Vakil and P.R. Brahmananda, *Planning for a Shortage Economy,* Vora and Co., Bombay, 1952, p. 10.
11. B.A. Chansarkar, *Models for Planning in India,* Himalaya Publishing House, Bombay, 1983, p. 27.
12. J.C. Kumarappa, *Economy of Permanence,* A.B. Sarva Seva Sangh, Varanasi, 1957, p. 189.
13. S.N. Agarwala, *The Gandhian Plan,* Padma Publications, Bombay, 1944, p. 36.
14. A.H. Hauson, *The Process of Planning: Study of India's Five Year Plans 1950-64,* Oxford University Press, London, 1966, p. 43.
15. V.T. Krishnamachari, *op. cit.,* pp. 36-37.
16. *Ibid.,* p. 40.
17. *Ibid.,* pp. 40-41.
18. *Ibid.,* pp. 41-43.
19. *Ibid.,* pp. 43-44.

20. *Ibid.*, pp. 44-45.
21. *Ibid.*, pp. 45-46.
22. Induction Material, Planning Commission, Internal Work Study Unit, 1988, p. 7.
23. Commission on Centre-State Relations, Government of India, New Delhi, 1988, p. 363.
24. Mary Parmar, *Development Planning in India*, Reliance Publishing House, New Delhi, 1992, p. 36.
25. Induction Material, *op. cit.*, pp. 7-15.
26. Commission on Centre-State Relations, *op. cit.*, p. 363.
27. P.B. Desai, *Planning in India*, Vikas, Ghaziabad, 1979, p. 31.
28. Bidyanath Misra, *Capitalism, Socialism, and Planning*, Oxford and IBH Publishing Co., New Delhi, 1972, pp. 199-200.
29. *Ibid.*, p. 200.
30. *Ibid.*
31. The Planning Process, Government of India, Planning Commission, New Delhi, 1963, p. 15.
32. Bidyanath Misra, *op. cit.*, pp. 202-203.
33. *Ibid.*, p. 204.
34. Fourth Five Year Plan 1969-74, Government of India, Planning Commission, p. 3.
35. Speech on the Third Plan to the All India Congress Committee Meeting in Raipur on October 30, 1960.
36. Inaugural Speech, Congress Planning Sub-Committee Report on the Ooty Seminar, All India Congress Committee, New Delhi, May 30-June 5, 1959, p. 47.
37. Gunnar Myrdal, *Asian Drama: An Inquiry into Poverty of Nations*, The Penguin Press, London, 1968, p. 805.
38. Bidyanath Misra, *op. cit.*, p. 206.
39. *Ibid.*, pp. 206-208.
40. First Five Year Plan: A Draft Outline, July, 1951, p. 256.
41. These administrative discretionary controls to: *(a)* capital issues controls, *(b)* licensing of new enterprises and of large extensions of existing ones, *(c)* foreign exchange allocations, and import and export controls, and *(d)* price and physical controls.
42. Gunnar Myrdal, *op. cit.*, p. 908.
43. The Planning Process, *op. cit.*, p. 10.
44. Bidyanath Misra, *op. cit.*, p. 214.

4

Decentralised Planning: An Overview

Introduction

The decentralisation of planning in India follows different impulses and has taken several routes. As a result, the concept of planning at the different level means different things to different people. This diversity is also reflected in the content of planning and the processes of plan implementation advocated[1].

One group of thinkers and activists advocates local level planning and people's participation because of their idealized view of Indian villages as more or less self-contained communities. This view was most forcefully expressed by Gandhi. Gandhian workers have to translate the concept of self-reliant 'village republics' into practice. The chief merit of Gandhian approach is the stress on self-reliance. Even this concept of decentralisation could not overcome the stratification of rural society and fragmented and fractional regional and local politics. Besides, links between the village and the rest of the world are too strong to be wished away and the influence of the outside world has proved to be overpowering. Gandhians had to face the basic issue of harmonising conflicting interests in a scarcity-ridden, inegalitarian society[2].

The next group of thankers advocated administrative, decentralisation, allowing lower units of administration to take decisions in order to ensure better identification of area specific projects, and proper coordination of economic activities. To bring them closer to genuine decentralisation local level planning activities were responded and the approach was termed "comprehensive". However, it is unrealistic to reproduce a local planning system on the lines of national or even state plans because of linkages which spill over local boundaries, economics of scale and the indivisibility of several projects. In practise such decentralised efforts largely intailed loose administrative coordination and entrusting certain 'agency' functions to the lower units of administration. Self-reliance was totally neglected and, the involvement of beneficiaries degenerated into the domination of the local elite through its control of popular institutions[3].

The third view is more selective. It concentrates more on the development of the rural poor and is based on two assumptions: that activities relevant for the poor are determined by specific characteristics of disadvantaged groups in different places and, therefore, should be location specific and that economic activities aimed at helping the poor will only be successful when the poor have sufficient control over local political institutions or can create their own political lobby. Thus, the organisation of the poor to generate demand and make claims on scare resources is considered part and parcel of local level planning[4].

In fact, change in the concept of decentralisation from administrative decentralisation to democratic decentralisation necessitated revamping of the planning machinery and the planning process[5].

Decentralised Planning: Conceptual Framework

With the publication of report of the Working Group on District Planning (1984), the concept of decentralised planning has become somewhat synonymous with the concept of District Planning, which may not be very appropriate. Decentralised planning connotes a better perception of the need of local areas, makes better informed decision-making possible, gives a greater voice in decision-making to the people for whom the development is meant, and serves to achieve better coordination and integration among programmes enabling the felt needs of the people to be taken into account. District planning is a kind of area based sub-State planning and arises from the need to supplement the national and the State plans with a more detailed examination of the resource, problems and potentials of local areas. The local area is accepted as the District and the investment programmes are tailored accordingly. It is similar to that of area planning which assumes that the District is a sub-State decision-making unit within the system of multi-level planning. Therefore, in the process of decentralised planning, one lower level after the State is represented by planning at the District. Whether that is the most appropriate level and unit of planning and whether further tiers of planning are needed to answer fully the requirements of decentralised planning are to be determined by the constraints in the administrative system, paucity of required basic data and qualified personnel to undertake planning on a systematic basis[6].

Decentralised planning is a system through which planning process is brought close to the people, who are the ultimate target of the development. It is a multi-level planning system in which, planning is attempted at different politico-administrative and executive levels, so that there is greater integration between the developmental needs and priorities of smaller areas (micro-regions) and different socio-economic classes with the regional, sub-national and national level development policies and goals. Decentralised planning is neither a substitute to centralised planning nor an exclusive bottom-up process of planning. It is in fact a two-way process which begins at both top-level (national or state level) as well as grassroots level (local level) simultaneously, and merge with each other at a point below which centralised planning becomes irrelevant and above which micro-planning is meaningless. This point can be identified at the district level as it is the cutting edge of the development administration. While national planning provides policy perspective for national growth pattern and resources to achieve them, the State (sub-national planning) provides regional development objectives in consonance with national policies and goals. The micro-level planning begins with the analysis of the needs of the people as well as small areas (local-level) and demand for future and provides a framework which rationalises and integrates them with the State and national goals[7]. Thus, the conceptual framework of the decentralised planning system as emerging for the country is depicted in Figure 4.1.

Figure-4.1

Conceptual Framework for Decentralised Planning

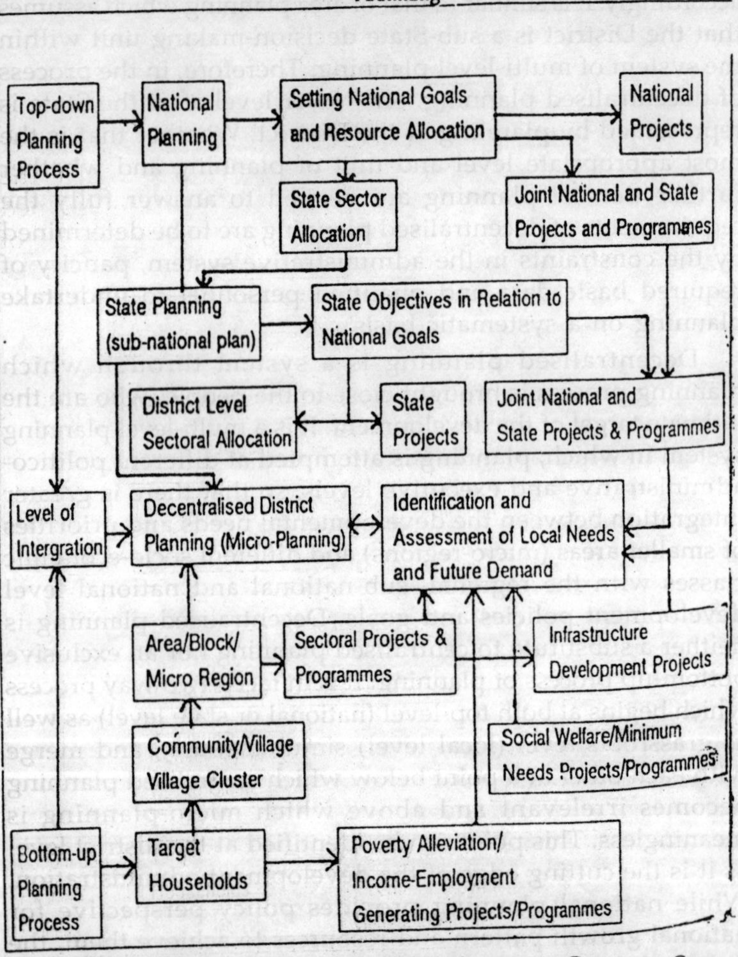

Source: B.K. Thapliyal,"Decentralised Planning: Concept, Scope and Methodology", *Journal of Rural Development*, Vol. 9, No. 6, 1990, p.996.

Decentralised planning can also be defined as "planning at different levels" or "multi-level planning". This may consist of planning at National level, State level, District level, Block level, Panchayat level or could be planning for a region.

In order to understand the concept of decentralisation of planning, we must first understand why decentralisation of planning is necessary in the country like India? A simple answer to this question would be that decentralisation is needed in order to counteract the evils of a highly centralised type of planning and decision-making. The centralised type of planning cannot adequately take care of all the requirements at different territorial and sectoral levels of the planning process. The task of planning requires not only the formulation of a broad policy framework but also specification of the details of this framework. A specification of details would be possible only in the light of relevant information and data. This kind of information is more readily available 'on the spot'. Planning has, therefore, to move closer to those levels where better informed decision-making would be possible. When planning thus get decentralised, it would tend to become more area-specific that is, it would be possible to establish close complimentarity between development schemes and local potentials, problems and priorities[8].

Centralised planning results in lags between development and the utilization of resources and capacities. These lags can be considerably reduced in decentralised planning[9].

The planning, process cannot succeed purely on bureaucratic lines. Active participation, are needed if planning and implementation are to succeed. Participation of people can be achieved only if planning is carried to the lower sub-national levels. Thus decentralisation is needed for effective mobilization of public participation[10].

Further, in developing countries like India characterised by inter-regional disparities in development and heterogen its in social structure, the problems of poverty and unemployment are "area-specific" and "group-specific" and demand a decentralised approach towards their solution[11].

Lastly, it has been established that decentralised planning ensures better spatial convergence and sequencing of inter-related activities and optimisation of investments[12].

In a broader sense, the move towards decentralised planning is the reaction to the following present day procedural aspects of centralised planning:

(*a*) Carrying out the theoretical and applied exercise at the national level by the Planning Commission which has the overall responsibility for the planning process including formulation of national plans and the outlays of the State plans;

(*b*) Determining at the centre the share of the public and the private sector outlays in relation to the suitable objectives of the growth of the country;

(*c*) Procedures followed for discussing the stratiqies, priorities, outlays (both of the Central and State plans) financing and implementation;

(*d*) Approval of sectoral outlays of the state plans by the Planning Commission right up to the last insignificant head of development; and

(*e*) Imposition of Central Sector and centrally-sponsored schemes without any discussions at Working Group meetings with the State Teams[13].

The above discussion provides us a conceptual framework for decentralisation of planning process. The decentralisation of planning process requires certain conditions to be met, if it is to successful. In this context, it may be noted that:

(*a*) Mere delegation of some powers and functions to sub-national units does not achieve all that is required;

(*b*) Genuine popular involvement in the process of planning is absolutely necessary. "In another words, participation of people at every stage and trusting the people is an indispensable precondition for bringing any kind of radical change in society"; and

(*c*) The roles of different agencies should be properly defined. Duplication should be avoided. It is necessary to clarify the work to be done at different levels and to indicate how their work is integrated with that of the Planning Commission.

In fact, the extent of decentralisation in the planning process needed for a country and the context of that decentralisation would depend on the problems and needs, perceptions and value systems of the country. The decentralisation of planning procedures are determined largely by the country's situation, its socio-political climate and its "development setting". Thus the concept of decentralised planning system has to be designed for the specific situations and cannot be generalised.

The conceptual framework for decentralised planning clearly indicates that micro-level planning (district planning) is the most important link in the whole system of decentralised planning because this is not only the cutting edge of administration but also the most appropriate level of planning where a suitable mechanism for distributive aspect can meaningfully be built into the development planning and also could be integrated with the overall growth system of the state and the nation[14].

Based on the objectives of the decentralised planning, there are three important components of the district planning. These are growth, equity and quality of life. Growth-oriented planning is essential area based approach which includes development of local resource potential and basic infrastructure to maximise production in all sectors of the economy. Equity-oriented planning is a target group approach in which identification of weaker sections of the society followed by creation of income and employment generating opportunities and/or transfer of the production assets and skills to the target people are dovetailed in the planning process. The third component, which is focused on the provision of social amenities and minimum needs that are essential for improving the living conditions and, therefore, achieving quality of life is community-oriented planning. Integration of all these three components on a geo-physical and socio-economic spatial plan-framework leads to the Integrated Rural-Urban Development Planning and provides a framework for 'district planning'[15]. The conceptual framework for district planning thus emerging can be visualised as depicted in Figure 4.2

Figure-4.2

CONCEPTUAL FRAMEWORK FOR DISTRICT PLANNING

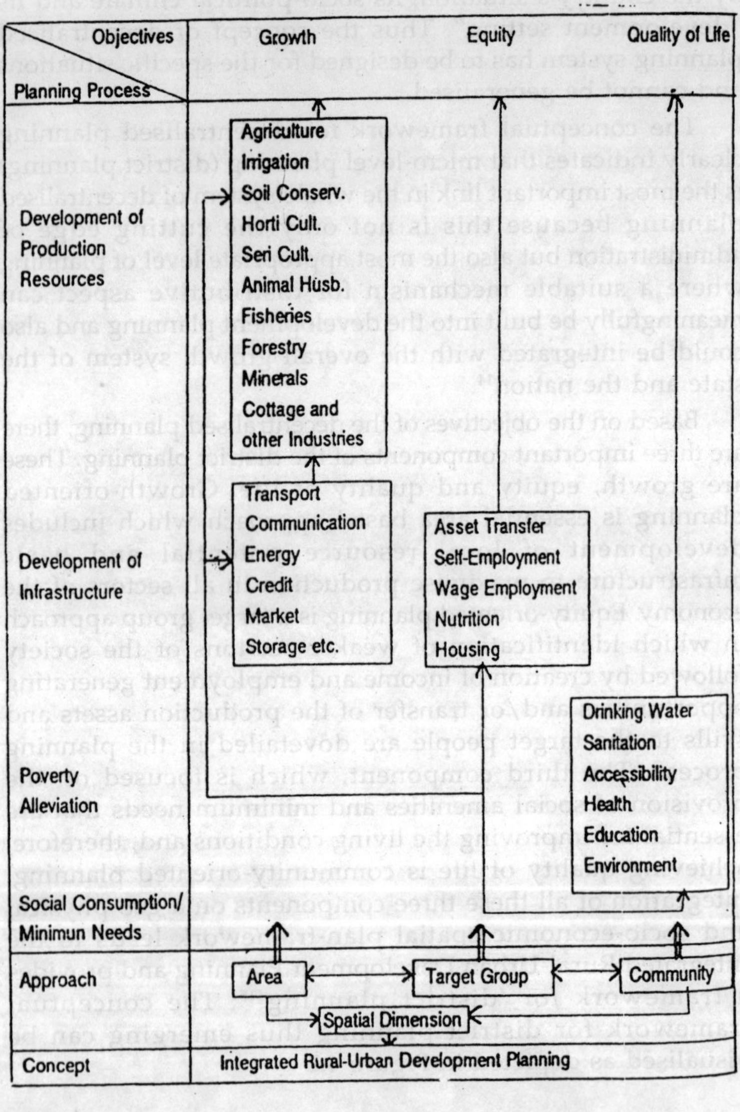

Source: B.K. Thapliyal,"Decentralised Planning: Concept, Scope and Methodology", *Journal of Rural Development*, Vol. 9, No. 6, 1990, p. 998.

Approach to Decentralised Planning

The approach to decentralised planning are still in a formative stage. There are, no doubt, many conceptual and methodological issues which are still un-resolved. This is a continuous process with various dimensions[16].

The Expert Group meeting on decentralised planning convened by Lal Bahadur Shastri National Academy of Administration, June 1990, considered the question of 'approach to decentralised planning' in detail. Dr. D.M. Nanjundappa in this meeting, bring out the areas of conflict and the issues which are still unresolved e.g. bringing out a conformity between national priorities and State priorities, taking the planning further below the district level either to a homogeneous resource region or to block/mandal level with the primary objective of removing regional imbalances. The Group recommended for covering 'Local Sector' below the district: a level where a particular activity or scheme/project can be formulated and implemented successfully. The Group observed that one of the most difficult approaches under decentralised planning was one of securing integration of schemes in a consistent planning framework[17].

The integration is needed in terms of the activities which are inter-dependent within the same sector and among the different sectors. While, even the existing sectoral programmes do take into account the needs of local people and target groups, generate employment opportunities, they include programmes for development of infrastructure and provide the resource as per needs, but they do not consider the resource potential and needs of the area by involving the local people in the planning process. Hence, it is necessary to consider integration of materials and the products of the area considered more integration of materials and the products of the area considered more appropriate for sustaining the development. This would mean taking into account forward and backward linkages, rural-urban linkages and need and resource linkages[18].

From the Figure 4.3, it could seen that the present system of planning is basically vertical planning where the process moves from top to bottom where policies and sectoral outlays move from National level to State level and from State level to District level. The area of operation, however, gets widened even now when we move from National level to State level to bottom because apart from the special plan (tied and untied) funds, the districts receive large amount of funds through centrally sponsored schemes (like IRDP and several poverty alleviation and other programmes) and also funds from institutional source like banks, voluntary agencies etc. The system of planning is, however, basically a sectoral planning (i.e. development of agriculture and allied activities, industries, education, health etc.). The proposed system of multi-level planning is a combination of both top down and bottom up planning and also widens the area of activity at the district level by including additional area and need based schemes. This expands the horizontal base at village level and provides a new point of integration of top down and bottom up planning at district level. This represents the integration of planning process from top to bottom which is not present in present planning process.

Decentralised Planning in India

Decentralised planning is not a new concept in India and goes back to 1951. It has, however, been limited to sectoral programmes at lower administrative levels rather than comprehensive planning for units below the Centre or State[19]. While planning at the national and state levels are well organised and established, planning at the micro-level was initiated with the introduction of Community Development Programme for which a vast decentralised network of development administration was created by dividing the whole country into more than five thousand blocks. It was also contemplated that these development units will be responsible for preparing village production plans and by aggregating them at the block level, formulating block plans. Though the contents of these plans were restricted to a few village level activities, nevertheless, it was a worthwhile exercise. This process, somehow did not last long as the CD Programme itself dwindled and ultimately faded away towards the end of the sixties[20].

Figure-4.3

INTEGRATION OF PLANNING PROCESS

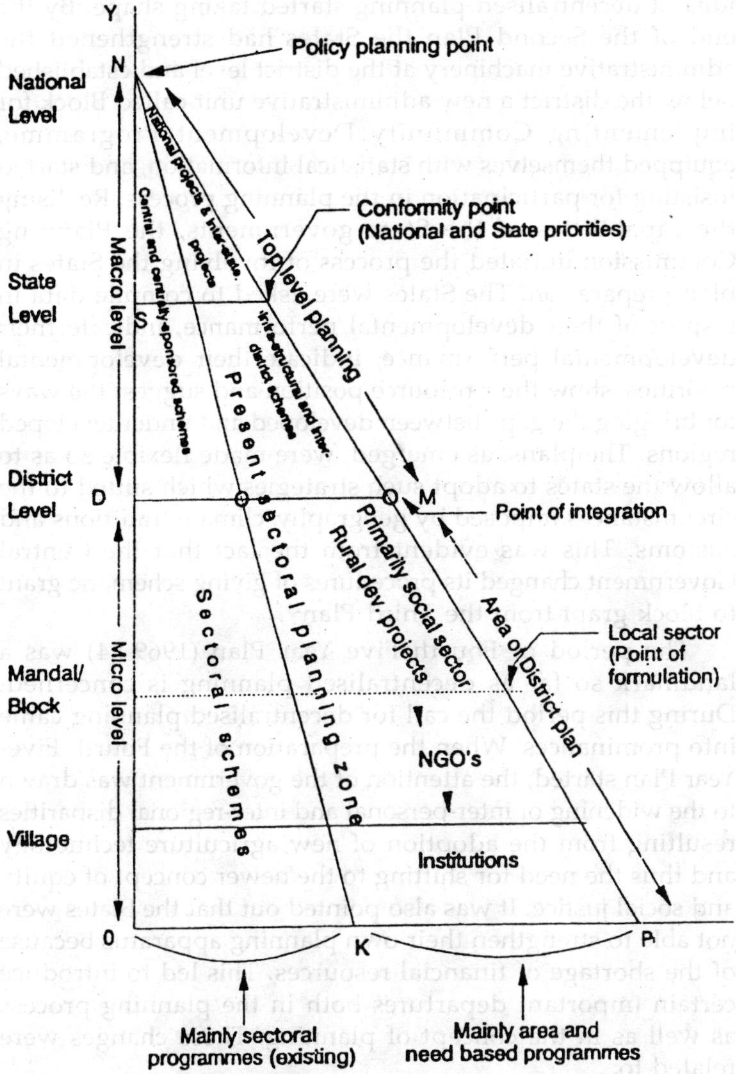

Source: C.S. Prasad,"District Planning: An Approach to Decentralised Planning", *The Administrator*, Vol. XXXVI, July-September, 1991, p. 44.

Another attempt in this direction was made during the period of Third Five-Year Plan and three Annual Plans (1961-66 and 1966-67, 1967-68 and 1968-69). It was here that the idea of decentralised planning started taking shape. By the end of the Second Plan the States had strengthened the administrative machinery at the district level and established below the district a new administrative unit called Block for implementing Community Development Programme, equipped themselves with statistical information, and started insisting for participation in the planning process. Realising the capabilities of the State governments, the Planning Commission initiated the process of involving the States in plan preparation. The States were asked to compile data in respect of their developmental performance, indicate their developmental performance, indicate their developmental priorities, show their resource position and suggest the ways for bringing the gaps between developed and underdeveloped regions. The plans, as emerged, were made flexible so as to allow the states to adopt such strategies which suited to the circumstances imposed by geography, climate traditions and customs. This was evident from the fact that the Central Government changed its procedures of giving schematic grant to block grant from the Third Plan[21].

The period of Fourth Five Year Plan (1969-74) was a landmark so far as decentralised planning is concerned. During this period the call for decentralised planning came into prominances. When the preparation of the Fourth Five-Year Plan started, the attention of the government was drawn to the widening of inter-personal and inter-regional disparities resulting from the adoption of new agriculture technology and thus the need for shifting to the newer concept of equity and social justice. It was also pointed out that the States were not able to strengthen their own planning apparatus because of the shortage of financial resources. This led to introduce certain important departures both in the planning process as well as in the concept of planning. These changes were related to:

(i) the pattern of devolution of plan funds to the state level embodying in it a measure of weightage to backward States,

(ii) emphasis on wide diffusion of initiative. decision making and participation, and

(iii) initiative for strengthening the planning apparatus at the State level, through a centrally sponsored scheme, so as to enable them to share the responsibilities[22].

The draft report on Fourth Five Year Plan (1969) emphasised district planning and provided detailed guidelines. Simultaneously, the Planning Commission initiated 20 Pilot-Projects for 'planning growth centres' in 18 States of the country with an aim to evolve area development planning methodologies using 'growth centre' model to suit different geo-climatic and socio-economic conditions of the country. This attempt also did not succeed in establishing district planning process in its real sense[23].

From Fifth Five Year Plan till the Seventh Five Year Plan (1985-90), it became possible to consolidate the gains of previous efforts for decentralised planning. By this time, it became clear that isolated efforted for decentralised planning would not be sufficient and that to make it functional it would need to be strengthened by organizational support. The capabilities for decentralised planning have to be constantly built up, the right procedures and suitable structures have to be evolved and necessary administrative and technical changes have to be evolved and necessary administrative and technical changes have to be affected. The important actions related to:

(i) expanding of the centrally sponsored scheme for strengthening planning machinery at appropriate levels,

(ii) emergence of a broad consensus that the district should be the functional unit for decentralised planning,

(iii) establishment of appropriate budgeting and reappropriation procedures, and

(iv) strengthening of Panchayati Raj Institutions (PRIs) for facilitating people's participation in plan formulation and implementation[24].

The review of the past attempts on district and lower level planning indicate that for quite sometime efforts are being made in this regard in some parts of the country, most of which are ad hoc and partial in nature. A serious effort to initiate district planning in its totality is still a distant dream because of various organizational as well as policy factors[25]. The G.V.K. Rao Committee also pointed the same.

Thus, the evolution of decentralised planning process in India is based on gradual step by step approach. One significant point that emerges from above analysis is that it was the Government of India, the Planning Commission which took the initiative for decentralising planning process so as to enable the State Governments to share the responsibilities. Though, the State Governments have started preparing their own Five-Year and Annual Plans, it is national planning that occupies even now a pre-eminent position in the planning process and the Commission (in effect the Government of India) influences the planning priorities of the States. There are at least three ways through which the Central Government can influence the planning process at the State level. These are:

- *(i)* allocation of Central resources, particularly the quantum of Central assistance to States;
- *(ii)* the distribution of Central investments among the different States; and
- *(iii)* the regulatory measures for channelising private and institutional capital through licensing and preferential lending policies[26].

Summing up

The nature and pattern of decentralised planning in India are varied because of the variety of institutions and practices in different states. There is a lack of uniformity in regard to social conditions, political compulsions and institutional structures. The constraints on decentralised planning are varied and many. Some of the important ones are: Political vis-à-vis lack of decentralisation of power, Administrative-Infrastructural inadequacies, Financial, Geo-physical constraints and social i.e. Bottlenecks imposed by the human resources.

Decentralised planning is not as simplistic as it looks on

paper. Capabilities have to built up, suitable structures have to be evolved, changes have to be brought about in the administrative, technical and political arena. Equally important is kindling the zeal and enthusiasm of the people. But the most important agents to make decentralised planning a success, is the political and administrative will to decentralise powers to the lower levels.

There have been frequent attempts to decentralised planning. However, the failure of most of these plans and programmes suggests a crucial omission. Decentralised planning has never gained real acceptance in important quarters. In principle, the central administration has accepted the idea of decentralisation but plan functions have not been delegated accordingly and the overwhelming central financial power remains without effective links between planners and politicians at various levels the entire responsibility has been left to officials and technical departments, who would like to retain tight control over their counterparts at lower levels. There is no evidence that local bureaucrats, technical hands, politicians or people have carried out any systematic planning, nor has any sustained effort been made to persuade them. More powerful, wealthy, and better entrenched groups have contained to siphon the benefits meant for the masses. Only the Block level planning exercise has any scope for comprehensive planning.

In fact, few real efforts to decentralised planning have been made and that these were marred by: *(i)* the financial predominance of the centre; and *(ii)* the highly centralised administration. Due to this the problems have largely remained unsolved.

While decentralised planning, and role of administrator and public participation appear to be operational matters requiring understanding, awareness, and procedures; in reality it is a far more complex process best with greater problems now than ever before. It deserves to be understood and pursued vigorously both as a value in itself and as a means of achieving societal ends because the success of micro-level planning depends heavily on relationships at different levels of public authority. The implications of multi-level planning have to be spelled out in order to make decentralisation a success.

The crucial importance of decentralised planning for a balanced and meaningful development of our country has been recognised since the very beginning of the planning era. But it has not been easy concept for operationalisation due to various constraints. Now the majority of the States have introduced the decentralised planning to their planning process. Indepth study of the decentralised planning reveal that block Planning should form the hub of this process and the decentralised planning, which is till now confined only to the district, must percolate down to the block and panchayat level. The experience gained during the last four decades of planning has demonstrated that merely wishing for decentralised planning would not be enough. To be successful; it has to be backed up by sound practices. The capabilities for decentralised planning have to be assiduously built up, the right procedures and suitable structures have to be evolved and necessary technical and administrative changes, including attitudinal changes have to be brought about among bureaucrats and in all those associated with this process. If these changes are not brought, then tall proclamations made in the Five Year Plans about introduction of dynamism in the planning process through Decentralised planning are going to remain, what they have been rhetoric for the galleries.

REFERENCES

1. V.S. Vyas, Anil Bhatt and S.M. Shah, *Decentralised Planning in India,* Oxford & IBH Publishing Co., New Delhi, 1985, p. 1.
2. *Ibid.,* p. 1.
3. *Ibid.,* pp. 1-2.
4. *Ibid.,* p. 2.
5. N.R. Inamdar and V.K. Keshire, *District Planning in India: A Case Study of Maharashtra,* Oxford and IBH Publishing Co., New Delhi, 1986, p. 15.
6. D.M. Nanjundappa, "Concepts, Approaches and Techniques of Decentralised Planning" in B.N. Yugandhar and Amitava

Mukherjee (ed.), *Readings in Decentralised Planning*, Concept, New Delhi, 1991, pp. 14-15.

7. B.K. Thapliyal, "Decentralised Planning: Concept Scope and Methodology", *Journal of Rural Development*, Vol. 9(6), 1990, pp. 995-996.
8. R.P. Mishra and K.V. Sundaram "Multi-Level Planning", in Moonis Raza (ed.), *Regional Development*, Heritage Publishers, New Delhi, 1988, p. 68.
9. *Ibid.*, p. 69.
10. *Ibid.*
11. *Ibid.*
12. *Ibid.*
13. D.M. Nanjunadappa, *op. cit.*, p. 18.
14. B.K. Thapliyal, *op. cit.*, p. 16.
15. *Ibid.*
16. D.M. Nanjundappa, *op. cit.*, p. 16.
17. C.S. Prasad, 'District Planning: An Approach to Decentralised Planning', *The Administrator*, Vol. XXXVI, July-Sep. 1991, p. 44.
18. *Ibid.*, p. 45.
19. V.S. Vyas, Anil Bhatt and S.M. Shah, *op. cit.*, p. 3.
20. B.K. Thapliyal, *op. cit.*, p. 997.
21. K.B. Srivastava, 'Management of Rural Development in India: The Case of Decentralised Planning', *Journal of Rural Development*, Vol. 9(2), p. 39.
22. *Ibid.*, p. 40.
23. B.K. Thapliyal, *op. cit.*, p. 998.
24. K.B. Srivastava, *op.cit.*, p. 40.
25. B.K. Thapliyal, *op. cit.*, p. 999.
26. V. Nath, 'Regional Planning in the National Plan', *Artha Vijnana*, Vol. 9, 1967, p. 60.

5

Committees and Commissions

Although the ideas of 'grass-roots planning' and 'planning from below' have their basis in Gandhian thought, attempts at crystallizing these ideals into concrete administrative and political structure have been emphasised since Independence. Recognising the importance of democratic institutions at the grass-root level, the Indian Constitution has laid down in the Article 40 of the Part-IV of the Directive Principles of State Policy that the State shall take steps to organise village Panchayats and endow them with such powers and authority as may be necessary to enable them to function as units of self-government.

The ideas of 'decentralised planning', 'planning from below', 'people's participation in planning', 'multi-level planning' etc. have been mentioned time and again in the Five Year Plan documents. But decentralisation of the planning process was more pronounced only from the Fourth Five Year Plan (1969-74). The concept of decentralised planning virtually goes back to 1953 when the Community Development (CD) programme was launched by the Government of India, motivated by the need and desire for decentralised economic development. As a part of this exercise, the State Governments were requested in 1954 to prepare district and village plans.

Subsequently, in the late fifties, the Panchayati Raj institutions came into being at the district and lower levels of administration to provide an institutional base for people's active participation and involvement in development.

Balwantrai Mehta Committee

The Balwantrai Mehta Committee was appointed on 16th January, 1957. The recommendations of the Mehta Committee, brought under the title "Report of the Team for the Study of Community Projects and National Extension Service". The Team recommended the establishment of a three tier structure for Panchayati Raj Institutions. The Committee recommended constitution of statutory elected local bodies with the necessary resources, power, and authority developed on them and a decentralised administrative system working under their control. It also recommended that the basic unit of democratic decentralisation should be located at the block/samiti level. The Committee envisaged directly elected Panchayats for a village or group of villages, an executive body called Panchayat Samiti for a block with directly elected and co-opted members and an advisory body called Zila Parishad at the district level constituted indirectly, mainly through ex-officio members from lower tier and others with the Collector as Chairman.[2] The National Development Council accepted the recommendations of a three-tier system of democratic decentralisation for development administration.

The Panchayat Samitis, within a jurisdiction co-extensive with a development block were entrusted all these development tasks which the block was to undertake under the CDP. More specially, these included development of agriculture in all its aspects, animal husbandry, rural industries, public health, primary education, social welfare and maintenance of statistics. It was also to be an agent of the state government in executing special schemes of development entrusted to it.[3]

To enable them to discharge their developmental functions, the samities were assigned specific sources of revenue like a percentage of land revenue, cess on land revenue, profession taxes, proceeds from tolls and bases, etc. In addition, the State Government were expected to provide conditional and/or unconditional grants-in-aid. And finally, all Central and State funds spent in the block areas were to be assigned to the Panchayat Samitis to be spent by it either directly or indirectly. The Samitis were to have a budget which has to be approved by the Zila Parishad. Thus the Panchayati Samitis were given resources and assigned developmental functions and were thus expected to formulate block plans on the basis of people's need which their (indirectly) elected composition was expected to ensure. To implement their plans the Samitis were given administrative powers over the technical extension officers who were to be under the administrative and operational control of their Chief Administrative Officers. All States and Union Territories have enacted laws for the establishment of Panchayati Raj Institutions except the State of Meghalaya, Mizoram, Nagaland and Union Territory of Lakshadweep.

But decentralised planning under the Panchayati Raj Institutions was not much of success due to many debilitating factors—political, financial, functional and administrative. When the basic premise of Panchayati Raj Institutions as units of self-government was lost, these institutions also lost their capability to fulfil the promise of development.

As far as decentralised planned development is concerned we could not achieve much. To rectify this defect and to improve the working of democratic institutions at the district and lower levels, the Government of India appointed a committee headed by Asoka Mehta in December 1977.[4]

Asoka Mehta Committee

The second most important Committee was set up in 1977 after the Janata Party came into power at the Centre. The short-lived Janata Government, while appointing the Asoka Mehta Committee, stated its exact purpose: "The Government accords the highest priority to rural development, so as to increase agricultural production, create employment, eradicate poverty, and bring about an all-round improvement in the rural economy. The Government considers that the maximum degree of decentralisation, both in planning and implementation, is necessary for the attainment of these objectives. It has accordingly been decided, in consultation with the State Government and Union Territories, to set up a Committee to enquire into the working of the Panchayati Raj Institutions, and to suggest measures to strengthen them, so as to enable a decentralised system of planning and development to be effective".[5]

The committee had the following terms of reference:—

1. To review the existing situation regarding democratic decentralisation in the States and the Union Territories, and the working of the Panchayati Raj Institutions from the district to the village levels, so as to identify short-comings and defects. In particular, to examine the working of these institutions in respect of—*(a)* Mobilisation of resources, *(b)* Planning and implementation of schemes for rural development in an objective and optimal manner, and in looking after the interests of the weaker sections of society.
2. To examine the methods of constituting the Panchayati Raj Institutions, including the system of elections, and to assess their effect on the performance of the Panchayati Raj System.
3. To suggest the role of Panchayati Raj Institutions, and the objectives which could be attained through them, for integrated rural development in the future.
4. To suggest measures for reorganizing the Panchayati Raj System, and removing the shortcomings and defects, with a view to enable these institutions to fulfil their future role.
5. To recommend the form and content of the relationship that should exist between the Panchayati Raj Institutions, the official administrative machinery, and the Cooperative and Voluntary Institutions involved in rural development.
6. To make such other recommendations, including those on financial matter, as may be necessary to ensure adequate availability of funds for the discharge of the responsibilities that may be entrusted to the Panchayati Raj Institutions.[6]

The committee submitted its report on 17th August, 1978. The Asoka Mehta Committee gave primacy to the district as the basic unit of decentralisation which was a fundamental departure from the system that had developed following the Balwant Rai Mehta Committee recommendations of making the block and Panchayat Samiti as the key units of decentralisation. The Asoka Mehta Committee assigned practically no role to block. It suggested a two-tier Panchayati Raj structure comprising the Zila Parishad at district level and Mandal Panchayats at the sub-block level with a jurisdiction over a number of villages and covering a population of 15,000 to 20,000. The existing block level Panchayat Samitis were to be converted into "non-statutory executive committees of Zila Parishads and when the Mandal Panchayats become active, most of their functions would be taken up by the Mandal Panchayats".[7]

The Mandal Panchayats, the Asoka Mehta Committee suggested would comprise directly elected members and representatives of Farmer's Service Society with provisions for representation of women and of Scheduled Castes and Tribes.

As regards planning, their roles were seen as implementation and promotion. They were to be responsible for implementation of the schemes and projects assigned by Zila Parishad. They would also "play a promotional role activating community action, build up organisation and project formulation". To enable them to function effectively, the Mandal Panchayats should have "purposive work allocation and transfer of money component alongwith the functions assigned to them for implementation". Thus, the Mandal Panchayat was visualised as essentially an implementing authority with clear demarcation of functions and financial resources. Their role in plan formulation was to be supplementary to the Zila Parishad role: "...the Mandal Panchayats...would have a key role in supplying the necessary information about the various schemes and suggest the potential areas of development as well as their requirements to the Zila Parishad... The planning unit at the district level should take note of the views articulated by the Mandal Panchayats from time to time".[8]

Asoka Mehta Committee[9] made thirteen recommendations regarding planning. These were:—

1. With the district as the strategic level for economic planning, the Zila Parishad should be made responsible for planning at the district level. The appreciation of the total resources, the credit availability and the necessary strategy formulation covering several blocks

would be feasible at the district level. An elected Zila Parishad would also provide the much needed correctives to the techno-economic plans. The production and employment programmes prepared at the block level will fit into the totality of the plan.

2. A professionally qualified team should be stationed at the district level for preparation of district plans. The composition of this group would be on the lines suggested by the Expert Group on Block Level Planning. While formulatinf the plans, the expertise of the district level staff should take into account a cross section of all shades of public opinion relevant to the district.
3. The State Government would have to provide continuous assistance in the process of district planning. It would have to ensure that the national objectives relating to weaker sections are pursued by the Panchayati Raj Institutions. They will also have to provide the financial and physical parameters as well as technical expertise to the technical group. It should also ensure equitable allocation of resources and fixation of long-range priorities.
4. The district plan prepared by the technical group would be placed before the "committee of the whole" of the Zila Parishad where the MPs, MLAs and MLCs are also members.
5. The State Government should provide necessary machinery for examining the district plans to enable formulation of the State Plans. It should also hold a dialogue with the Zila Parishad in this regard.
6. The district planning should take care of urban-rural continuum. The district plan should also analyse data on growth points and growth centres in order to provide for necessary economic flows.
7. Intensive exploitation of new opportunities of resources earmarked for the Weaker Section should be a part of the plan process itself. The District Social Justice Committee will be of considerable help in this regard.

8. The on-going exercise of District Planning should also take into account the formulation of sound projects and short-term action plans covering areas of specific endowments, poverty belts and specific targets groups.
9. In order to avoid the problem of non-implementation and non-absorption of the many "delivery systems" which are already functioning, the several implementation components of all the local-level projects should be analysed in advance and greater attention should be paid towards synchronization and orchestration of the activities of the project-level functionaries of the different disciplines. Coherent activity analysis, standardized micro-project plans including flow-charts of good, services and functionaries will also have to be prepared so that the Mandal Panchayat can play an effective role in administrative coordination and institutional supervision.
10. At present, some districts are too large to facilitate drawing up of composite plans keeping in view, among others, the guidelines of compactness, effectivity, manageability and the number of representatives in the Zila Parishad, smaller districts would be desirable.
11. To begin with, the Mandal Panchayats may be limited to implementation and promotional roles, but they would have a key role in supplying the necessary information about the various schemes and suggest the potential areas of development as well as their requirements to the Zila Parishad. They would have to play this role on a continuing basis and not merely by holding a meeting to consider the draft plan or sending their comments on it to the Zila Parishad. The planning unit at the district level should take note of the views articulated by the Mandal Panchayats from time to time.
12. The total credit inflow for agricultural development is expected to rise significantly in the years to come. The Panchayati Raj Institutions should, therefore, pay greater attention to the institutional finance rather than

concentrating on budgetary sources as in the past. This would be possible only if the Panchayati Raj Institutions pay due attention to ensuring greater responsiveness in project implementation by ascertaining the views of the beneficiaries since those require considerable people's participation like Revised Minimum Needs Programme.

13. The Panchayati Raj Institutions should not only be regarded as a forum for obtaining the views of people's representatives but, in due course, they should become capable of planning for themselves within the resources available to them.

Unlike the Balwant Rai Mehta Committee, the Asoka Mehta Committee recommended direct elections to the Zila Parishads with reservations for Scheduled Castes, Tribes. For planning purposes, the recommendations was for setting up a Committee of the whole Zila Parishad with MLAs, MLCs and MPs from the area as ex-officio members. The Zila Parishad was to be the basic unit of decentralisation with a comprehensive range of developmental responsibilities. In fact the Committee went even further by recommending that all developmental functions related to the districts be transferred from the jurisdiction of State Governments to the Zila Parishads. The Zila Parishads, to be able to perform the developmental role, were to have all the staff under the supervision of the Parishad. The Parishad was also to have financial powers and earmarked devolution of funds for developmental purposes. In short, the Committee visualized a separate tier of development administration below the State with comprehensive and clearly defined developmental, administrative, financial and legislative functions.[10] The committee reviews the progress already made regarding planning from below. Since planning requires a lot of expertise the Committee suggests that there should be a professionally qualified team at the district level for the preparation of district plans, a thing which has been woefully lacking all these years. In conceives the ideas of a "planning cell" at district level, which should consist of an economist/ statistician, cartographer/geographer, agronomist, engineer (irrigation/civil), industries officer (small and cottage industries) and a credit planning officer. This cell will have to work in collaboration with all the other district level officers who will be under the Zila Parishad and who are closely associated with the problems of development. To begin with, the role of Mandal Panchayats would essentially be one of promotion and implementation of plan projects and schemes. The Committee also covers other aspects of decentralised planning such as formulation appraisal, implementation and monitoring of projects.[11]

The recommendations of the Asoka Mehta Committee, although fairly radical, did not find much favour with the State Governments. To discuss the committee's report a conference of Chief Ministers was held in 1979. The discussion led to the preparation of a model bill to ensure uniformity in the Panchayati Raj System. As things stand today only a few States, most notably Karnataka, has gone ahead and implemented the Panchayati Raj System on the lines recommended by the Asoka Mehta Committee. Perhaps a greater involvements of the Centre in the process, including possibly an amendment to the constitution to ensure democratic decentralisation upto at least the district level may be necessary. In fact, two Constitutional Amendment Bill (64th and 65th) were prepared one by the Congress and the other by the National-Front Government with this broad objective in view.[12]

Dantwala Committee

In November 1977, the Planning Commission appointed a Working Group under the chairmanship of Prof. M.L. Dantwala to draw up guidelines for block level planning. The Working Group submitted its report in 1978. The report grew out for

(a) generating employment,
(b) assuring basic minimum needs,
(c) effective spatial planning for rural socio-economic infrastructure, and
(d) promoting equity. In fact, the Committee in its report enumerated these, inter alia, as the goal of the back-level planning.[13]

The Working Group on Block Level Planning observed that below the State or Divisional Level, District and Block Level Planning are visualised as part of the same exercise, in as much as block level planning would also be attending to all aspects of District Planning. The main purpose of Block Level Planning, is to accelerate the process of the decentralisation, which would help to speed up the development process and also improve it qualitatively. The Block Level Planning is complementary to District Planning. Block being sufficiently small in terms of area and population, could enable intimate contact and understanding between the planners, implementers and the people.[14]

The Working Group held the view that the remoteness of the planning agencies from the area of implementation and the vastness of geographical coverage had been hampering the matching of sectoral financial allocations with location specific needs as well as potential and getting in the way of proper distribution of the gains of development. The idea behind block level planning was to accelerate the process of decentralisation with the hope that a more systematic planning effort with a smaller coverage would not only help to speed up the development process but also improve it qualitatively in the sense of making it more responsive to the needs of the community.[15]

The Working Group was of the opinion that the block-level planning should not be treated as an isolated exercise. It should be treated as a link in a hierarchy of levels from a cluster of villages below the block level to the district, regional and state level. While finalizing its recommendations for submission before the Asoka Mehta Committee, the Working Group recognised the block as a unit of planning. It was regarded as a certain community of interests as was sufficiently small in terms of area and population to enable intimate contact and understanding between the planners, those responsible for implementation of the plan, and the people. At the same time it could also provide an observation platform close to the beneficiary group and help to understand more clearly the felt needs of the people and factors inhibiting the uplift of the weaker sections,to ascertain area—specific physical and human resources potential, to identify constraints inhibiting socio-economic and technological growth and to expand the area of people's participation and implementation of plans.[16]

In the opinion of the Working Group, the range of planning functions at the block level was determined by the size of its geographical limits and a quantitative and qualitative appraisal of its human and material resources. And as such one of the first tasks of block-level planning should, therefore, be to demarcate the block-level planning canvas from that of the district and state level functions. The plan at the block level, on the one hand, should be related to the plans of the districts and the State, and on the other, to the plans for the clusters of the villages within the block. Without sacrificing planning efficiency, the Working Group gave only an indicative idea of activities which could be planned and executed at the block level.

The Dantwala Committee found that expertise was absent at the block level. It stated that the "the present staffing pattern at the block is mainly tuned to implementation tasks and not so much towards planning functions. The set-up basically consists of a Block Development Officer who is assisted by five Extension Officers, each in the fields of agriculture, animal husbandry, co-operation, Panchayats and rural industries. The other staff consists of an observer, a social education organiser, a Progress Assistant and VLWs. In the block, there are also Veterinary Stockmen, a Medical Officer, a Sanitary Inspector and a Lady Health Visitor, some of them with the necessary supporting staff. In some states there is also an Extension Officer for programmes relating to women and children. Thus, it may be seen that the staffing pattern at the block level is essentially meant for getting the development programmes implemented in the field. There is a Progress Assistant who keeps record of the plan programmes and their progress and assists the BDO in sending regular progress reports. Beyond this, there is no other person assisting the BDO in the planning functions".[17]

However, despite recognising the absence of planning personnel at the block level, the Dantwala Committee did not recommend that such personnel should be inducted at the block level. Realising that planning skills were scarce it recommended the constitution of a District Planning Cell which would be entrusted with the task of formulating both district and block plans: "...we are visualizing the planning team located in the district essentially as a peripatetic team, which will move down to the selected blocks and prepare the block level plans in association with the BDO, the Panchayati Samiti, Voluntary agencies and other concerned persons at the block level". Thus, the Committee was trying to introduce block-level planning without changing block level administration. It laid greater stress on the technical tasks, like collection of data and assessment of public opinion, to the block administration. This emphasis on the technical aspect of planning led it to underplay the roles of both the administration and the Panchayat Samitis. In the absence of popular involvement, the Dantwala Committee's recommendations fall far short of what is understood by "grass-roots planning" though its strength lay in its attempt at upgrading planning capabilities at the sub-state levels.[18]

Hanumantha Rao Committee

The crucial importance of decentralised planning for a balanced, acceptable and meaningful development of our country has been recognised since the beginning of the planning era. But it has not been an easy concept for operationalisation due to various constraints, like the inadequacy of the planning machinery itself and the lack of a uniform enthusiasm on the part of the states who were required to operationalise it. Even though the Planning Commission issued some guidelines on district planning to the states in 1969, the idea could not catch up because many states were not ready to undertake it. But with the changes in the orientation and structure of development planning over the last two decades. In the view of the developments that have taken place since 1969 and as the methodology for local level planning has considerably evolved all over the world, there was need to take a fresh look at the whole matter. This Working Group was, therefore, set up by the planning commission for this purpose in September, 1982 and the Working Group submitted its report in May 1984.[19]

The Working Group was set up with the objectives of defining the scope, content and procedure of district planning and to establish links between planning from the block to the State levels.

The idea of comprehensive decentralised planning was again taken up by the C.H. Hanumantha Rao Committee: This working group reiterated the earlier recommendation that "block planning should also be entrusted to District Planning Team". The purpose of block planning should be, in addition to the goals of district planning of which the blocks are components, the reduction of intra-district disparities for which the district planners should develop suitable intra-district variation indicators. However, unlike the Dantwala Committee, the working group recommended the introduction of planning personnel at the block level also.[20]

The Working Group on district planning has inter alia, recommended that: *(a)* for decentralised planning to make headway, institutional mechanism have to be made more broad-based with the active involvement of local representatives and endowed with a greater degree of autonomy in local decision making, *(b)* the Panchayati Raj Institutions and other local government institutions should play a crucial role in the district planning process.[21]

The Working Group, as per its terms of reference, laid down the functions of district planning bodies as follows:

(a) crystallization of local needs and objectives,
(b) taking stock of the natural and human endowments,
(c) listing and mapping of amenities,
(d) formulation of district plans,
(e) formulation of policies, programmes and priorities,
(f) coordinated implementation, and
(g) monitoring and review of district plans and programmes.

For these tasks the working group suggested the setting up of a broad-based District Planning Body Comprising of representatives from the Zila Parishad, Panchayat Samitis, Municipalities/Corporations, MLAs, and MPs from the district, prominent personalities, workers and entrepreneurs, representatives, bank representatives etc. The total membership of the body could be around fifty. In addition to the District Planning Body there should be a smaller Executive Body or Steering Committee with the District Collector as the Chairman, the Chief Planning Officer as the Member-Secretary and other members drawn from important officers of development departments and agencies. The working group therefore was a de facto group. It favoured the transfer of the planning function to a body other than the Zila Parishad till the time Zila Parishads become effective and active. These non-elected bodies, the group suggested, may be constituted by an executive order. To aid the District Planning Body in technical matters, the Working Group further recommended that there should be a District Planning Cell/Office headed by a Chief Planning Officer with a status next to that of the District Collector. The Chief Planning Officer should be specially trained in regional/area planning and should be assisted by a team of experts from various disciplines and subject areas. The group also suggested the strengthening of the Collector's role and clear definition of financial and administrative powers for the district level government and adequate disaggregation of outlay according to districts. Thus the working group made for reaching recommendations on the technical and administrative aspects of district planning.[22]

CAARD

The Committee to Review the Existing Administrative Arrangements for Rural Development and Poverty Alleviation Programmes, headed by Dr. G.V.K. Rao, former Member Planning Commission (March, 1985) also went into the question of decentralised planning and supported the recommendation of the Working Group. More specially, it endorsed the Working Groups' recommendation for setting up District Planning Bodies and the suggestions for decentralisation of financial and administrative powers.

The CAARD deit in detail about the decentralised planning and has recommended *inter alia* that:

(*a*) The crucial development should be the major component of district planning, though the District Plan should encompass the total activity of the district,

(*b*) The district should be the basic unit for policy planning and programme implementation. The Zila Parishad, should, therefore, became the principal body for management of all development programmes which can be handled at that level,

(c) Panchayati Raj Institutions at the district level and below should be assigned an important role in respect of planning, implementation, and monitoring of rural development programmes,

(d) The State level may have to be transferred to the district level for effective decentralised district planning,

(e) In order to give some—and manoeuvrability in planning and decision-making, it is necessary to make some funds available at the disposal of the District Planning Body which are not tried to any departmental schemes and which may be used towards small schemes meant for the local priorities, needs, and aspirations of the local community.[23]

The CAARD also recommended the setting up a State Development Council (on the analogy of the National Development Council) so that district and state plans can be brought into a common framework. Thus, once again fairly detailed suggestions were made to restructure the district administrative machinery in order to handle the gigantic task of developmental planning.

Sarkaria Commission

Another Commission which looked into the working of the Economic and Social Planning was the Sarkaria Commission. The Commission on Centre-State Relations, which is popularly known as the Sarkaria Commission, was set up by the Minister of Home Affairs, Government of India on 9th June, 1983 under the chairmanship of R.S. Sarkaria.

The terms of reference of the Commission were as under: "The Commission will examine and review the working of the existing arrangements between the Union and States in regard to powers, functions and responsibilities in all sphere and recommend such changes or other measures as may be appropriate.

In examining and reviewing the working of the existing arrangements between the Union and States and making recommendations as to the changes and measures needed, the commission will keep in view the social and economic developments that have taken place over the years and have due regard to the scheme and framework of the constitution which the founding fathers have so sedulously designed to protect the independence and ensure the unity and integrity of the country which is of paramount importance for promoting the welfare of the people."[24]

Though the Commission was constituted to look into the basic question of Centre-State relations, yet, in its report, the Commission devoted considerable attention on the question of decentralisation of power and planning process. The Commission recommended that the institutions like Zila Parishads and elected Municipal Corporations need to be significantly strengthened both financially and functionally.

REFERENCES

1. Involvement of the People in the Planning Process, Planning Commission, 1989, p. 14.
2. *Ibid.*
3. Pranab Banerji, "Grass Roots Planning", in S.N. Mishra, *Course Material of Tenth Course on Development Through Participation (July 25-August 5, 1994)*, IIPA, p. 42.
4. *Ibid.*
5. S.N. Mishra, *Rural Development and Panchayati Raj*, Concept Publishing Company, New Delhi, 1981, p. 44.
6. Govt. of India, *Report of the Committee on Panchayati Raj Institutions*, Government of India, Ministry of Agriculture and Irrigation, Department of Rural Development, New Delhi, 1978, pp. iii-v.
7. Pranab Banerji, *op. cit.*, p. 45.
8. *Ibid.*
9. Report of the Committee on Panchayati Raj Institutions, *op. cit.*, pp. 185-187.
10. Pranab Banerji, *op. cit.*, p. 32.
11. S.N. Mishra, *op. cit.*, p. 61.
12. Pranab Banerji, *op. cit.*, p. 32.
13. *Ibid.*, p. 44.

14. V.S. Singh, "Decentralised Planning Need Reorientation", *Yojana,* July 1-15, 1987, p. 5.
15. S.N. Mishra, *op. cit.*, p. 66.
16. *Ibid.*
17. Pranab Banerji, *op. cit.*, p. 45.
18. *Ibid.*, p. 45.
19. Govt. of India, *Report of the Working Group on District Planning,* Government of India, Planning Commission, May, 1984, Foreward.
20. Pranab Banerji, *op. cit.*, p. 46.
21. Involvement of the People in the Planning Process, *op. cit.*, p. 19.
22. Pranab Banerji, *op. cit.*, pp. 35-36.
23. Involvement of People in the Planning Process, *op. cit.*, p. 20.
24. Govt. of India, *Commission on Centre-State Relationship Report,* Government of India, Ministry of Home Affairs, New Delhi 1988, p. III.

6

Decentralised Planning: Operational Experience from States

The decentralised planning as a concept has been much more talked about than practiced. The style of planning in this country has been planning from the top and the people in general have never been involved in the process. The Indian experience of decentralised planning presents a mosaic of varying pattern and different hues. Although the need for decentralisation of the planning process is recognised, the progress achieved in this direction is not uniform and different states have achieved decentralisation in varying degrees and in different ways.

In the succeeding pages, a detailed account of the functioning of decentralised planning in the states have been presented. An attempt has also been made to discuss the various factors which hinder the proper functioning of decentralised planning in these states.

Andhra Pradesh

Andhra Pradesh may be said to be outstanding in the field of regional planning. An extremely high status was accorded to this aspect of planning in the Fifth Plan. Andhra Pradesh delineated three distinct conventional regions—Telangana, Rayalaseema and Coastal Andhra. The approach followed by the state was essentially regional. It had, therefore, the advantage of being able to dovetail its regional plans into the state plan. Each of these regions had "broad characteristics required for being treated as a distinct physical planning region in itself".[1] District Planning was included in regional planning itself and was given an important status in the Fifth Plan.

The initial stages of plan work (both Five Year and Annual) i.e. setting out plan policies, broad objective and considering alternative targets were the responsibility of the Planning Secretary. The Technical Departments and Working Groups were involved only in the last function mentioned above. At the macro state, projections of the rate of growth of income and commodity target—setting were handled jointly by the Planning and Technical Department. Regional development and planning was the area of the three Regional Development Committees and Planning Department.[2]

Sectoral planning in the case of annual plan was mainly done by the Planning Department. This agency decided on the number of sectors for the planning and the sectoral allocation of investment and outlay. It involved the Technical Departments in fixing sectoral targets and monitoring sectoral planning. At the project stage, it was generally the Technical Departments which handled the work of project formulation, location, size, submission, sectoral composition and the number to be selected. The State Planning Board also had a say in the matter of the selection of projects. The Planning Department monitored projects planning and guided the location of projects.[3]

At the regional stage of planning, three agencies participated, viz., the Planning Department, State Planning Board and the Regional Planning Committees of the State Planning Board. The Regional Planning Committees determined the targets for the regions. The Regional Development Committees came into the picture only in the case of Five-Year Plans. The organisations and individuals involved in district planning were the Planning Department and the Zila Parishads, and the Block Development and District Planning Officers. However, for all practical purposes, the main work of planning for the district was carried out at the State level itself.[4]

Administrative Reforms Commission's recommendations led to the setting up of the Andhra Pradesh State Planning Board on 1st January, 1974. The State Government set up the Board to function as an expert body. At the time of its constitution, the Board had a total strength of fourteen. It consisted of the Chief Minister as Chairman, the Deputy Chief Minister as Deputy Chairman, and the Secretary to the Government incharge of Planning as ex-officio Member Secretary. Its ex-officio members were Ministers in charge of Planning and Finance, the Chief Secretary to the Government, the ex-officio Development Commissioners, and three Chairmen of the Regional Planning and Development Committees. Its part-time members were five experts, mainly economists. In October 1974, the Constitution of the Board underwent some changes. The designation of the Deputy Chairman was changed to that of the Vice-Chairman and the Finance Minister was changed to that of the Vice-Chairman and the Finance Minister was assigned to this post in the place of the Deputy Chief Minister. The Minister for Health and Medical Welfare, the Chief Secretary to the Government and the ex-officio Development Commissioner—who replaced the Finance and Planning Ministers—were appointed ex-officio members. The remaining members continued as before, but the total strength was reduced to thirteen.[5]

The State Government was of the opinion that it was "necessary to ensure that the State Planning Board is assisted by bodies consisting of people's representatives and constituted for different areas and that such bodies are represented on the Planning Board itself."[6] Therefore, in January 1974, it set up Planning and Development Committees for the three regions in the State, namely. The Telangana Planning and Development Committee, for the districts of Adilabad, Karimnagar, Khammam including, Bhadrachalam and Nugur Taluks, Hyderabad, Mahabubnagar, Medak, Nalagonda, Nizamabad and Warangal. The Rayalaseema Planning and Development Committee for the districts of Anantapur, Chittor, Cuddapah and Kurnool; and the Coastal Andhra Planning and Development Committee for the districts of East Godavari, Guntur, Krishna, Nellore, Prakasam, Srikakulam, Visakhapatnam and West Godavàri.[7]

The Chairmen of these Committees were ex-officio members of the State Planning Board (to ensure co-ordination between the two agencies). The members of these committees were members of the Legislative Assembly. The State Planning Board appointed three part-time members to each of these Committees to render expert advice. A Deputy Secretary of the Planning Department was appointed Secretary of each of these Committees. The tenure of the members of the Committees was two years. The State Planning Board functioned like a Cabinet Sub-Committee with a sprinkling of a few outside experts. It was set up mainly as a result of the States 6 point formula.[8]

A few legislation was passed in 1986 which came into force on 15-1-1987. Under the new Act, 22 Zila Praja Parishads (ZPPs) have been constituted with Chairmen directly elected for each by all registered voters. Under the new structure of Panchayati Raj set up, the ZPPs have been entrusted, among other things, with the task of preparation of District Plans. Besides, District Development Review Boards (DDRBs), have been constituted for monitoring the developmental activities in the District. The Chairmen of ZPP, all MLAs, and MPs, who are members of ZPPs are its members with District Collector as Member Secretary and a nominated Minister as Chairman.

It was decided to formulate the Seventh Five Year Plan (1985-90) of the States on the basis of District Plans. Instructions were issued to the District Collectors to formulate district plans, which may reflect the thinking at the district level, and the felt needs of the local areas, and may consist of three parts: Part-I indicating the resources position, Part-II giving the plan outline and its broad objectives, parameters, physical targets, etc. and Part-III giving the details of the schemes. Accordingly, District Plans have been prepared for the Seventh Plan period for all the districts of the State. But these plans could not be integrated into the State's Seventh Five Year Plan 'due to several uncertainties'. At present, only district segments of Annual Plans are being prepared and communicated to the DDRBs for information and reference at the district level.

Although there has been no provision of 'United Funds' as such, the State Government has introduced some innovations during 1984-85. A provision of Rs. 23.00 crores was made at the rate of Rs. 1 crore for each of the 23 districts in the State. The same amount was recommended for 1988-89 also. This amount which is in the nature of 'United funds' was released to help finance 'crucial balancing investments'. The works undertaken under this scheme involved non-recurring capital expenditure. The DDRBs formulated schemes for each district which are under various stages of implementation, and nearing completion. The other innovation in the new scheme called 'Telugu Grammena Kranti Patham'. This is a scheme for execution of a large number of small works in the countryside not requiring substantial skills, but locally relevant and significant, which reflect felt needs of the people directly by the people through 'Telugu Srama Dalams'. At the instance of the Planning Commission, the State Government has selected three districts (East Godavari, Adilabád and Anantpur) for the preparation of district plan on pilot basis.

Arunachal Pradesh

In Arunachal Pradesh, District Planning Boards have been set up. However, decision regarding the manner of operationalising the concept of decentralised planning in the state has yet to be taken.

Assam

Decentralised planning has been introduced in Assam from April 1, 1986. Under this, plans will be formulated at the sub-divisional level. Decentralised planning will take into consideration the needs, the potentials and levels of development of different sub-divisions.[9]

A decentralised planning machinery at the state headquarters and planning cells at the district level have been created. In the plain districts of Assam, the unit of decentralised planning will be the sub-division. Each sub-division will consist of sub-divisional planning and development council. A core group constituted at the headquarter level will also draft the sub-divisional plan. All schemes will be grouped at state level schemes or as sub-divisional level schemes.[10]

The state level schemes are those which will benefit the state as a whole and not any individual sub-division. These schemes will, however, cover generation of power, major and medium industries, professional and technical educational institutions, research and training programmes, inland water transport, state highways and the like. The sub-divisional schemes, on the other hand, will comprise of agriculture production, minor irrigation, fisheries, community development, social forestry, IRDP, RLEGP, NREP, rural roads, elementary education, rural development, rural employment etc. The responsibility of preparation of sub-divisional plan will vest with the sub-divisional planning and development council. The sub-divisional planning cell will be composed of a Cabinet Minister as Chairman, Deputy Commissioner as Vice-Chairman, District Planning Officer, Senior Planning Officer, S.D.O. (Civil), MPs and MLAs of the sub-divisions, Secretary of the Mahakuma Parishad, Chairman of the Town Committee, Project Director DRDA, sub-divisional Planning Officer, one representative from University or research institute, lead bank, State planning and development—all as members.[11]

A core group for each district as a professional body, will make draft sub-plan from time to time. The sub-divisional planning initially will be taken up in all the plain districts of the state. Gradually it will be extended to other departments.[12]

Proposals from various departments outlining the programmes that they wish to implement and the funds required along with a list of location, specific schemes under each programme will be sent to district planning officer. The core group will then examine and scrutinise the proposals. This will emerge as a draft Annual sub-divisional plan for placing before the Sub-divisional Planning and Development Council. The core group will determine the inter-sectoral allocations and priorities of programmes and schemes as per needs and potentials of the sub-division. The Planning Development Department (PDD) will guide the core groups regarding the national and state priorities of development. The core groups will also consider the guidelines issued by various development departments.[13]

The PDD will scrutinise the draft Annual sub-divisional plan and will discuss the same at concerned authority level. The State Planning Board will approve the draft annual sub-divisional plans. The PDD will issue necessary working papers and agenda in this connection for consideration of the planning board. The draft annual sub-division plan will be integrated with the draft annual plan for the state level schemes which will then form the draft annual plan of the state. This will then be submitted along with the approval of the state cabinet to the Planning Commission. Sub-divisional plans will then be finalised after plan discussion with the Planning Commission. In the process of finalisation of sub-divisional plans, the orientation of priorities of the Planning Commission will be given due cognizance.

After the draft sub-divisional plans have been sent by the sub-divisional planning and development council to the PDD, the core group will start a detailed exercise for finalising the location of specific project to be implemented by various development departments. The Development Department will prepare detailed estimates of the schemes that have received approval of the sub-divisional planning and development councils.[14]

The sub-divisional Planning and Development Council will monitor the work of implementation undertaken by the respective development department. Consequent upon the adoption of sub-divisional planning in the state, responsibilities of the administrative departments as well as the heads of department will increase manifold. They will then be entrusted with the duty of planning overall strategy, formulate and issue guidelines, its follow up action, give technical advice, issue technical and administrative approval and supervise the implementation work of district development officials.[15]

Formation of sub-divisional planning and development councils will, however, exist without disturbing the prevailing process of planning and implementation of the tribal sub-plan or the integrated tribal development projects. The DRDAs will come under the guidance of the sub-divisional planning and development councils.[16]

Hence th- exercise has been termed as the grass-root planning. It will at present cover 31 Mahakuma Parishad of 16 districts in plain areas. This includes 135 development blocks, 711 village Panchayats and 21,995 inhabited villages of the state.[17]

Bihar

A high status was awarded to regional planning in the State's Plan. In fact, a balanced regional development was one of the priority objective of the Fifth Plan and perspective plan of Bihar. Regional Development Authorities were set up in Patna, Muzaffarpur in Gaya and Bhagalpur. These authorities were charged with the responsibility of ensuring the planned growth of the areas. Although the importance of regional planning was emphasised, it still remained a weak point in Bihar's planning effort.[18]

District Planning has been introduced in Bihar since 1985-86. District Planning Cells consisting of a District Planning Officer and some technical and ministerial staff has been created in all the districts of the state.

District Planning and Development Council (DPDC) with a Minister of State as its Chairman, and also Executive Committees headed by Divisional Commissioners to assist the DPDCs, have been set up. Whereas the DPDC is envisaged as a policy making body, the Executive Committee is entrusted with the work of formulation, implementation and review of various sectoral development programmes and schemes at the district level.

The District Administration has been instructed to prepare a District Profile incorporating necessary information required for planning. District officers have also been instructed to prepare Five Year Plans and Annual Plans for their districts as well as a Master Plan indicating the perspective for future growth. Adequate powers have also been delegated to the District Administration for the implementation of the District Plan schemes.

Planning and Development Department of the State Government organises training programmes for officers involved in the district planning in various institutions within and outside the State. It is proposed to give them field experience by posting them as BDOs.

Public participation is ensured through DPDC. The Zila Parishads are not active, but Panchayat Samities at the Block Level are very active.

Gujarat

Gujarat is one of the leading states which have attempted to decentralise the planning process. A very high status was accorded to regional planning in the perspective plan. The regional planning approach was adopted to achieve a balanced regional development. The purpose was to formulate "a plan for the spatial and temporal organisation of population and socio-economic activity in the State of Gujarat, consistent with regional objectives of harmonious physical optimum use and development of resources and of planned urban and rural development, with due regard to the objectives of the national plan".[19] The regions delineated were economic and three in number namely, Tribal areas; Drought prone areas; and Backward areas. The chief parameter of regional planning was the level of industrialisation.

The State also attached considerable importance to district planning. District Planning Boards (DPBs) have been set up in all the districts of the State. These Boards are headed by a Minister of the State Government. To make people's participation effective, DPBs have been made broad—based bodies and include people's representatives (MLAs, Presidents of Panchayats and representatives of municipal bodies) and also officials. DPBs are provided with a small complement of staff headed by District Planning Officer, which serves as the technical cell for the formulation of the district plans.

Plan schemes have been demarcated into State and District sector schemes. Twenty per cent of the district sector outlay is earmarked as 'united' (discretionary outlay) to be operated by District Planning Boards. Out of this 20%, 5% is given as incentive outlay to the District Planning Bodies who raise matching contribution varying between 25 to 50 per cent, depending upon the level of development of the district. This is a novel feature of the decentralised experiment being conducted in Gujarat. Guidelines have been issued by the State Government for the utilization of discretionary and incentive outlays. Within these broad guidelines, the District Planning Bodies have the discretion to choose schemes, to be financed with the discretionary and incentive outlays, depending upon the felt needs and priorities of the area concerned.

Haryana

To decentralised the planning process, at the district level, District Planning Advisory Boards were constituted "to give due weightage to the aspirations of the people and to bring the people in closer contact with the plan formulation process and implementation at various levels". District Planning Boards (DPBs) and Executive Committees have been set up in each district in December, 1986. The Boards had members of Parliament and Legislative Assembly, Chairmen of Zilla Parishads, Presidents of Municipal Committees and other knowledgeable persons in the district. In other words, they were managed by official and non-official members. The Deputy Commissioner served as Chairman, and the District Planning Officer as Secretary. The functions of the Board were to advise the district authorities on the priorities to be adopted and the programmes to be taken up for a systematic socio-economic development of the district, with due attention to the backward pockets and potential areas.[20]

In addition to the District Planning Advisory Boards, District Planning Committees were constituted in all the districts in the State. They consisted only of official members. They had three functions, namely,

(i) to assist in the formulation of long-term district perspective plans;

(ii) to help in evolving a short-term strategy (Five Year/ Annual plan) for a planned development of the district and to indicate programmes/schemes for an effective utilisation of resources; and

(iii) to review the progress and ensure the smooth implementation of plan schemes.[21]

A third organisation at the district level is the District Executive Council; it consisted of the Deputy Commissioner, District Planning Officer and the District Statistical Officer. The Council was responsible for the formulation of the District Development Plan. Thus, it appeared that Haryana had a very viable district planning machinery.[22]

Himachal Pradesh

The concept of decentralised planning has been accepted by the State Government and District Planning and Development Committees (DPDCs) has been constituted in the 10 districts of the State (except the tribal district of Kinnaur and Lahul and Spiti). Planning Cells have been created in the 10 districts, and have been assigned specific responsibilities. These cells are expected to become fully functional by the end of 1987-88. They are proposed to be further strengthened by providing the posts of experts in different disciplines, according to the guidelines issued by the Planning Commission. A comprehensive duty chart, which includes preparation of resource inventory and village level data inventory, has already been prepared. Nucleus budgets for district level plans have been provided for 10 districts of the State to be utilised by the Deputy Commissioners for local development works of importance with the approval of the DPDCs. The funds are allocated among the districts according to a formula which gives 60% weightage to population and 40% to area. In 1985-86, an outlay of Rs. 100 lakhs was provided as 'united funds' and the provision for 1987-88 was Rs. 375 lakhs. For 1988-89 also, Rs. 375 lakhs have been recommended.

At the instance of the Planning Commission, the State Government has identified three districts (Shimla, Mandi and Kangra) for the preparation of district plans on pilot basis.

Jammu and Kashmir

Jammu and Kashmir is a pioneer in district planning, and has taken long strides after the setting up of District Development Boards (DDBs) in the year 1986. The Deputy

Commissioner of each districts, who has been designated as District Development Commissioner, has been assigned the role of Chief Co-ordinator as the Chairman of the DDB. The DDB has Superintending Engineer of the district as Vice-Chairman, and all MLA and MLCs of the district, one representatives from amongst the elected Sarpanchs from each Block Development Board of the district and members nominated by the Government to give representation to weaker sections, backward areas and women, as members. Deputy Director, Planning (Statistics), is the Member-Secretary of the DDB. The DDB has been given full powers to determine plan priorities within the district and oversee the implementation of various development programmes in the district. The District Development Commissioner is in the overall charge of the development of the district, and exercises powers of major Head of development of the district, and exercises powers of major Head of Department for all the development departments functioning in the district, all such departments in the district being placed under his administrative and operational control. The DDB meets at least three times in a year. The first meeting is held in the beginning of the year for the formulation of the Annual Plan, the second meeting is held for the mid-term appraisal of the Plan and the third meeting is usually held to review the performance of the Annual Plan at the close of the year.

District Planning Cells have also been set up in each district to assist the District Development Commissioner in the formulation, implementation and monitoring of the district plan. These cells are headed by an officer of the rank of a Deputy Director. It is also proposed to strengthen these cells by induction of subject matter specialists like Credit Planner, Agronomist, Social Development Officer, Land Development Officer, etc.

The planning process has, in fact, been decentralised up to the block level and a sub-plan is drawn up for each block of the district. It is proposed to adopt the block as the primary unit of planning in the State. Till such time, however, as machinery for formulating the block plan comes into existence, this work has been entrusted to the district level planning machinery.

With the induction of block level planning, the total State plan is now broken up into three parts—the State level plan, the District level plan and the Block level plan. Detailed guidelines have been issued by the Government regarding the formulation of these plans.

The present procedure of determining the district outlays in the State is that once the plan outlays for the State are settled and sectoral provisions and priorities determined, the Heads of the Departments are required to communicate the break-up of state sector component and the district sector component of their sectoral plans according to the existing guidelines issued by the State Government. The proportion of the district sector component thus arrived at is distributed amongst the districts on the basis of three broad guiding factors viz., population, area and level of development or backwardness. The proportion of district sector component in the total State plan does not remain constant but varies from year to year. On an average, 40% to 45% of the total State plan is earmarked for district sector schemes every year.

Once the Planning Department Communicates to each District Development Commissioner the total outlay for the district plan together with sectoral break-up as well as broad priorities and guidelines, a detailed district plan is drawn up by the District Administration in consultation with the District Development Board. Since 1986-87, lumpsum outlays for five broad sectors of economy are being communicated to the District authorities on the basis of which District Development Boards apportion the outlays for each of the sectors and sub-sectors after taking into consideration needs, priorities and guidelines issued by Planning Department, etc. These five broad sectors are as under:

(i) Agriculture and Rural Development;

(ii) Industry and Commerce;

(iii) Power;

(iv) Transport and Communications; and

(v) Social and Community Services.

A formula has also been prescribed for the distribution of outlays among the blocks within the districts. The backwardness has been given due weightage in this formula to ensure adequate flow of funds to relatively more backward blocks.

A unique feature of district planning in Jammu and Kashmir is the review function performed by the State Cabinet. The entire Cabinet participates in a meeting with the DDB at the district headquarters or at any other place in the district to review the performance of the Annual Plan. Senior officers of the government, including Heads of the Departments, also participate in these meetings. The members of the Board are free to comment on the performance of the various departments. Such of the problems as may require immediate attention of the cabinet are resolved on the spot.

Karnataka

Karnataka initiated the district planning in 1978-79. With the establishment of Mandal Panchayats and Zila Parishads on April 1, 1987, Karnataka is now having three tier planning structure, i.e., State, Zila Parishad and Mandal Panchayat. The major objective of establishing these local government institutions is to decentralise decision-making process to the district and mandal levels. Government has identified the schemes which are to be operated at the State, Zila Parishad and Mandal Panchayat levels. The areas for planning at these levels have also been identified. The planning process has been drawn up so as to make the decentralised planning process really meaningful. For the purpose of plan formulation, instead of sector-wise or minor head-wise allocations, the Zila Parishads and Mandal Panchayats will be indicated a lumpsum allocation. This will allow full freedom to determine their priorities and draw up programmes accordingly. However, the Zila Parishads and Mandal Panchayats are required to earmark specified outlays for MNP, special component plan and tribal sub-plan. For the purpose of distribution of outlays between the Zila Parishads an objective criteria which given 50% for various indicators of level of development has been prescribed. Similar criteria is also adopted for determining the share of Mandal Panchayats in the district in order to ensure equitable spread of outlays and programmes between the Mandal Panchayats. Sanctioning, reappropriation and financial powers have also been duly delegated to Zila Parishads and Mandal Panchayats. Prior to the establishment of these institutions, no district head of the Department, except PWD officers, had the power of according technical sanction to any scheme. Under the Zila Parishad set up, these officers are given the power of according technical sanction to any scheme/project involving an outlay upto Rs. 2 lakhs. Zila Parishads are given the power of according administrative sanction for all the ongoing schemes and new schemes with an outlay upto Rs. 10 lakhs in each case. Zila Parishads and Mandal Panchayats are also given the power of reappropriation upto 10% of their approved budget.

Broadly speaking economic and social infrastructure is given priority. These include Health, Education, Roads and Veterinary services. But the production oriented sectors like Agriculture, Horticulture, Fisheries and even minor irrigation have not received similar consideration. Some schemes under cooperation, Soil and Water Conservation, Agriculture and Horticulture, have been dropped by all the Zila Parishads uniformally. Nominal or token provision for works is almost absent in Zila Parishad proposals. On the other hand, the requirements of each sector are fully assessed and provided.

At the organizational level, there is a District Planning Committee in each district comprising of Project Director, District Rural Development Society; General Manager, District Industries Centre; District Development Assistant, District Publicity Officer; District Statistical Officer and District Planning Officer (Member-Secretary), headed by the Deputy Commissioner. This body is responsible for the initiation of the first draft on district plan which is then placed before the District Development Council for approval (with or without modifications). The Council consists of all MPs, MLAs, MLCs of the district, the TDB Presidents and all officers of the district with the Deputy Commissioner as the Chairman.

Kerala

Kerala started to decentralise planning process in a phased manner. In the first phase, the district planning approach is being adopted for the formulation and implementation of schemes under the Special Component Plan (SCP) on the basis of the Scheduled Castes Habitat Survey carried out in all the districts of the state. Area with concentration of 10 or more scheduled caste households have been identified, and the basic data relating to each sub habitat collected. A plan for the development of all such identified habitats, and for the development of scheduled caste population has been drawn up for each district. The programmes covered by these plans account for nearly 12 per cent of the State Plan outlay.

District Development Councils (DDCs) at the district level and Block Development Committees at the block level have been constituted. District Planning Committees and Sectoral Planning Committees have also been set up.

A District Administration Act was enacted in 1979 with the object of bringing about a democratic and decentralised system of administration at the district level. The Act provides for an elected District Council, vested with the powers of administration in respect of matters enumerated in the First schedule to the Act. These cover a wide range of activities, including administration of land revenue and local resources mobilization. It is hoped that the implementation of this Act will help in the decentralisation of the planning process. The rules contemplated in the Act are yet to be framed.

The nucleus planning cells, consisting of a Junior Agronomist, an Assistant Executive Engineer and a Cartographer, created earlier, have since been abolished. The State Government is formulating proposals for the planning set up at the district level in accordance with the guidelines issued by the Planning Commission.

Madhya Pradesh

In Madhya Pradesh, no decision has yet been taken regarding the manner in which the concept of decentralised planning is to be operationalised in the State. District Planning Boards (DPBs), headed by a non-official, have been set up in 29 districts. The Collector of the district is the Secretary to the DPB.

Forty-Five posts of District Planning officers were

sanctioned under the scheme of the strengthening of the planning machinery at the district level.

An amount of Rs. 5.4 crores was provided for three Minimum Needs Programmes, namely, Water Supply, Elementary Education, and Roads, which was distributed to all the districts at the rate of Rs. 10 lakhs per district. The schemes under these programmes were sanctioned by the DPBs.

Maharashtra

Maharashtra has introduced decentralised planning process since the beginning of the Fifth-Five Year Plan. In the fifth plan of Maharashtra, regional planning received much importance. Regions were delineated on administrative and economic grounds. Bombay, Poona, Nagpur and Aurangabad were the administrative regions.

The most remarkable aspect of planning in Maharashtra was district planning. The government adopted in the principle of the district planning since the Fifth Five Year Plan and decided to consider the district as a unit of planning from 1972 onwards.

District Planning and Development councils (DPDCs) have been established in all the 30 districts of the State. The DPDCs is headed by the designated Minister and the District Collector is its member-Secretary. Other ministers/ministers of State from the state are co-chairmen, and the Divisional Commissioner is the Vice-Chairman. All the members of Parliament, Vidhan Sabha and Vidhan Parishad from the district, Presidents and Chief Executive Officers of the Zila Parishads, Mayor(s) of Municipal Corporation(s), if any, and one President each of the 'A' 'B' and 'C' class municipal councils in the district, chairman of the District Central Cooperative Bank, etc., are its Members. Fourteen non-official member, drawn from various fields, are also appointed on the DPDCs. Each DPDC has an Executive Committee. District Coordination Committees have also been set up under the chairmanship of the District Collector.

DPDC has been entrusted with the responsibility of the formulation of the district plan, taking into account the local needs and resources available, and to monitor and review the implementation of the district plan. The DPDC serve as an umbrella organisation for the plans of individual agencies, which are integrated into a district plan.

Planning Cells, consisting of District Planning officers, one Research Assistant, two statistical Assistants and other supporting staff exist in each district.

Since 1984-85, the state has been providing special allocation at the rate of Rs. 2 crores for each district for taking up small works, based on the felt-needs of the district, such as missing road links, C.D. works, small bridges, primary school rooms, Samaj Mandir, etc., each such work, casting not more than Rs. 3 lakhs, to be completed in one working season. The Seventh Plan provision for these programmes is Rs. 30 crores. These programmes are finalised by the DPDC in accordance with the guidelines issued by the State Government. These funds are over and above the normal district plan allocation made available to each DPDC. Necessary financial and other powers, have been delegated to the district officers for ensuring speedy implementation of these programmes. For 1988-89, an amount of Rs. 64 crores has been recommended as 'united funds'.

The State has also taken some steps to introduce block-level planning. Orders were issued to formulate block plans, within the district plan, for six selected blocks in the state on an experimental basis. However, not much headway could be made mainly because of limited planning capability at the district level.

A separate wing has been established in the Planning Department of the State Government for the purpose of coordination of district plans and allied matters.

The collector, as member-Secretary of the DPDC, plays the role of the Chief Coordinator. The progress of implementation of the programmes of every Department is reviewed in a monthly meeting of the DPDC or its Executive Committee, under the chairmanship of the minister in charge.

The Planning Department brings out an annual publication indicating the provisions finally decided for the Annual Plan of each district, and places it before the Legislature with other budget papers. The administrative Departments are required to make the release of budget provisions according to the district-wise and scheme-wise provisions indicated in this publication. Saving in any scheme or programme are utilised in the same district, for which the DPDC has been delegated the powers of reappropriation.

The State Government has itself stated that although district planning has been in operation in the State for the last 12 years, presently it tends to be only district budgeting. The planning process, starting with the collection of data relating to resource endowment, assessment of financial resources and determination of priorities, and culminating in the formulation of a comprehensive plan, has not been adopted. What happens mostly in that Departmental schemes are put together within the available financial ceiling, and are presented as a district plan. This has been so because of several factors, such as, lack of planning capabilities at the district level, the burden of the continuing schemes, the provision of reconciliation of the vertical plans (i.e., the Plans of line Departments) and horizontal plans (i.e., district Plans) etc. It is stated that attempt will now be made to prepare District Plans on more scientific lines.

Manipur

Manipur has a nucleus of planning staff consisting of a District Planning officer, an Assistant Research Officer, a Research Assistant, two Research Investigators and some supporting staff in each district. It is proposed to strengthen the Planning Cell in one of the district on a pilot basis, to begin with, by induction of an area/spatial planner/geographer and an economist/statistician/systems analyst with project appraisal background.

District Planning and Development Council (DPDC) has been constituted in each district. This body is headed by a Minister. There is no provision for an 'united fund' in the Seventh Plan of the State. An amount of Rs. 40 lakhs at the rate of Rs. 5 lakhs per district was provided for the Annual Plan 1987-88 as 'united fund' for the eight districts of Manipur, subject to State Government locating a saving of Rs. 40 lakhs, keeping in view factors like population, area and level of development of the district. It has further been suggested that the State Government may issue guidelines indicating the kind of schemes which can be taken up with the 'united fund'.

The Manipur (Hill Areas) District Council Act, 1971, was enacted by the Parliament. The Act extends to five districts of Manipur covering 9/10th area of the State. The objective of the Act is to bring about political consciousness among the tribal people for better administration by their own elected members, particularly for safeguarding their customs and usages and for ensuring their greater involvement in developmental activities.

Manipur has six Autonomous District councils in five hill districts, one of the districts having two councils. Each council consist of 18 elected members, and two nominated members for a term of five years. Each council elects its chairman from amongst elected members. There is a Chief Executive Officer appointed by the Governor from the Manipur Civil Service Grade I who functions as Ex-officio Secretary of the council. At the State level, there is a Hill Commissioner in charge of the district council. The District councils have no income of their own, and depend 100% on the grant-in-aid by the Government.

Meghalaya

District Planning and Development Councils (DPDCs) have been constituted for all the five districts of the State superseding the District Planning Boards constituted earlier. District Coordination Committees headed by Deputy Commissioner have also been set up. District Planning Officer is the Convenor of this Committee. The existing planning machinery, both at the State and the district levels, is inadequate and needs to be suitably strengthened. It is difficult to find suitable technical personnel in the State to strengthen the planning machinery.

There are three Autonomous District Councils in Meghalaya. In addition to the scheme formulated by the State in these council areas, funds are also allocated for developmental activities of the District councils for taking up the following kinds of schemes:

(*a*) Rural Communications such as construction of village roads, footpaths, etc.

(*b*) Rural Water Supply Schemes such as Ringwells, Water tanks, etc.

(*c*) Self-help schemes such as council's Buildings and Playgrounds.

Mizoram

There is practically no district planning in Mizoram. There is need for setting up a proper planning machinery at both the State and the district levels. During the Annual Plan 1986-87 discussions, it was suggested that the requirements of planning personnel at the State and the district levels need to be studied, and necessary proposals formulated.

Out of the three districts in Mizoram, the district of Chimtuipuri has three district councils, i.e., Pawai District Council, Lakher district Council and Chakma District Council. These Councils had so far been engaged in activities in five sectors, i.e. Road Communication, Sanitation, Water Supply, Art and culture, Forests. Later the sphere of activities of these councils has been enlarged by the Government.

Nagaland

Government of Nagaland has yet to initiate planning at the district level, although District Planning Boards (DPBs) have been set up in the State. The DPBs are headed by the Deputy Commissioner of the district. At sub-Divisional level, sub-Divisional Planning Boards have been set up in three Sub-Divisions, which are headed by Additional Deputy Commissioners. Similarly, at the village level, Village Development Boards have been set up in three Sub-Divisions, which are headed by Additional Deputy Commissioners. Similarly, at the village level, Village Development Boards have been set up. Planning Cells consisting of Planning officer and Assistant Planning officers have been set up, which require strengthening.

The State Government have introduced the system under which small schemes for meeting the felt-needs of the community are taken up through Block Development Officers and district Planning Boards. These schemes fall mainly under Forestry, Education, Health, Drinking Water, Sanitation, etc.

Orissa

Regional planning was accorded great importance in the Fifth Plan. Regions were delineated on economic grounds. District planning also received considerable attention in Orissa's Fifth Plan. District Development Boards (DDBs) with Collectors of the district as chairmen have been constituted in all the districts. These are District Planning committees (DPCs) headed by Collector, and also subject matter sub-Committees under the DPC to prepare sectoral plans.

The DDBs function as advisory bodies for plan formulation and review of the progress of implementation of the plan programmes. The DPC integrates the various sectoral plans and prepares a final district plan. There are Gram Panchayats at the Village level and also Block level Samities.

District Planning Machinery consists of the Chief Planning officer, a credit Planning officer and the supporting staff has been sanctioned.

Provision of 'united fund' has been made in the Seventh Plan. In January, 1986, the State Government issued instructions to all the Collectors regarding the utilisation of 'united fund'. These funds are placed at the disposal of the district Planning Committee for small but essential development works which cannot be accommodated within the district sectoral plans. The DPCs are required to formulate important programmes/schemes to fill in some essential gaps in the district and to meet some immediate needs of the people of the area. Since the amount is not tied to any sector, the DPCs are given full freedom in the choice of the programmes/ schemes of local importance.

Punjab

The State Government has accepted the concept of decentralisation of the Planning process as enunciated in the Report of the Working Group on District Planning and the

Seventh Plan document. District Planning Boards have been constituted in all the districts of the State.

Rajasthan

The State Government has accepted, in principle, the concept of decentralised planning. Regional planning in Rajasthan in the Fifth Plan. The parameter adopted for regional planning was the level of industrialisation. The regions in the State were delineated on economic grounds.

District planning was initiated in Rajasthan in the Fifth Plan period "in a limited way in respect of the Minimum Needs Programme sectors." District Planning Committees were set up in all the districts. District-wise financial allocation for the Minimum Needs Programme sectors and guideline for the preparation of plan proposals were sent to the District Collectors by the Planning Department. Provision of Rs. 270 lakhs as 'united fund' is made for district planning.

Sikkim

At present, there are District Coordination Committees in each district which are functioning under the chairmanship of a Cabinet Minister. Apart from this, no other action has so far been taken in regard to the district planning. Considering the small size of the State, the expenditure involved in creating a separate planning set up in each of the four small districts in the State and the paucity of suitable technical personnel, a view has been taken that it is not desirable to decentralise the planning process to the district level in the State. The planning machinery at the State level itself may be strengthened so that it can efficiently formulate integrated development plans for each of the four districts, keeping in view the resource potential and the specific needs of each district.

Tamil Nadu

District Planning was taken up very seriously in the State, for it was thought that the involvement of the people at the grassroots level would lead to the realisation of the macro objectives. In Tamil Nadu, "with the centralised aggregative planning machinery and techniques built up over the past four plan periods, the first task in local and area planning has been to create the minimum machinery for such an effort."[23]

Work on district planning began in March-April, 1972. One member of the Planning Commission was in charge of it. Thirteen District Planning Cells were set up in the thirteen Revenue Districts in the State. The thirteen District Planning officers were appointed. The District Planning officers were given training in the methodology of district planning for ten days by the State Planning Commission. The Chairman of the Task Force issued guidelines to the District Collectors. Each District Planning Cell was headed by a District Collector, who was assisted by a Planning Officer oriented in the techno-economic approach to planning, and by a Statistical officer at the District level. District Planning work was constantly monitored by the Secretary and the chairman of the Task Force.

Tripura

The thinking of the State Government in regard to decentralised planning has yet to crystallise. At present, there are three districts and nineteen blocks in the State. One-tier Panchayati Raj System at the village level is prevalent in the State (but there are Block Development Committees with non-official participation). The thinking in the State is to decentralize planning to the block level and have only two levels of planning, viz., Block and the State. But, the planning machinery is proposed to be set up only at the district level. This machinery will be utilised for the preparation of the block plans.

There is one Tribal Areas Autonomous District Council (TAADC) in Tripura. The Area of the Council consists of parts of three revenue districts of the State. The TAADC is administered by a Chief Executive Member, and a number of Executive Members who are elected members of the Council. The council has a Chief Executive councilor, assisted by a team of officers designated as Executive officers and Principal officers incharge of development departments like Animal Husbandry, Fisheries, Agriculture, Industry, Cooperation, Forests and Engineering.

The TAADC takes up schemes for primary education, agriculture, minor irrigation, fisheries, animal husbandry, forestry, etc. The TAADC gets funds in the form of a lumpsum grant out of the State's Annual Plan, and also share in agricultural income tax, professional tax, land revenue and forest royalty. It also gets funds by way of transfers by different departments of the State Government out of their plan funds.

Uttar Pradesh

Regional Planning received a very important place in the State's Fifth Plan. The parameter in terms of which regional planning was done were; Level of industrialisation, value of agricultural production, population density, and electricity consumption (infrastructure). Administrative and economic regions were delineated in the State. The regions delineated were: Hill Region, Western Region, Central Region, Eastern Region and Bundelkhand Region. The five economic regions were delineated by grouping contiguous districts having more or less similar geographic and climatic conditions, economic activity pattern, population density and agricultural conditions.

Two committees have been set up at the district level in the State. These are: *(i)* District Planning and Monitoring committee, and *(ii)* District Plan Coordination and Action Committee. The first committee is headed by a member of the council of ministers of the State, while the second one by the District Magistrate. In each of the districts, there is a district Economic officer, assisted by three Assistant Economists/Statistical officers and one Cartographic Assistant. This set-up has been in existence since 1982. All the State Plan schemes have been classified into State and District sector schemes. The State Government has also devised a formula for the allocation of divisible outlay among the districts, which, according to the State officials, was nearly 30%. The State had got a district plan formulated for the districts of Jhansi and Hardoi on a pilot project basis.

The State Government has taken various preliminary measures like setting up of district Planning bodies, disaggregation of outlays and devising of a formula for allocation of district-sector outlay among the districts, but the formulation of district plans, as advocated by the Working Group on District Planning, has not yet been taken up. The State Government had appointed a committee to go into various aspects of decentralised planning including the establishment of planning machinery at the district level. In addition to the above, the State government had also appointed another Committee to go into the question of simplifying the existing budgetary procedures and minimising delays in reappropriation of funds. This committee has recommended adoption of a single budgetary grant for departments and schemes under the district sector. Yet another committee, a high-level one, is looking into the question of planning set-up in the State. After a decision is taken on the recommendations of these committees, proposals for district planning machinery will be formulated, and steps will be taken for the formulation of district plans as advocated by the Working Group on District Planning.

West Bengal

Decentralised planning at the district and block levels was adopted in West-Bengal from 1985-86, the first year of the Seventh Plan. Decentralised planning in West Bengal means integrated district and block level planning. The idea is that all development programmes in an area, no matter which agency is operating them, should first be known to the local planning authorities, so that the various schemes under diverse rural development programmes may be formulated in the light of an analysis of the resource position and economic conditions of each block, and various schemes for urban development may be formulated in a co-ordinated manner for each urban areas, and then these block and municipality plans may be integrated into a district plan. Thus planning is starting from bottom[24].

The basic ideas underlying the State's decentralised planning concept is that the Government set up the requisite machinery at district and block levels in 1985-86. The machinery at the district levels has two-tier, one, the district planning and coordination council, and the other, its executive arm, the district planning committee. At the block level, the machinery is called the Block Planning Committee[25].

The District Planning and Coordination Councils (DPCCs) are headed by ministers who hail from the district concerned, while the vice-chairmen are the sarbadhipatis or heads of the Zilla Parishads. Other elected representatives of the district are also members, while the District Magistrates act as member secretaries[26].

The District Planning Committees (DPCs) are headed by sarbadhipatis of Zilla Parishads with District Magistrate's also working as member secretaries. The membership is drawn from Panchayat samities, chairmen of municipalities, representatives of statutory authorities functioning in the District and Government officials functioning at the district level. Teams of technical experts and administrative officials assist the functioning of these bodies.[27]

The planning committees at the block level are headed by Panchayat Samiti sabhadipatis, block development officer acting as the member-secretary. The membership is drawn from elected panchayat bodies and Government officials working at the block level. Teams of technical personnel and administrative officials also assist these committees.[28]

The bodies both at the district and block levels receive overall guidelines as to priorities of development and the funds may be available to them from various departments and the funds may be available to them from various departments of the Government like IRDP, NREP, RLEGP and Institutional funds, and critical gaps are bridged out of the 'United Funds'. Once the resource position is known, the planning process starts. The planning committee prepare plans and projects in the light of the resources to be available from the various agencies, but always bearing in mind that the projects will satisfy the felt needs of the people. The felt needs in each block or district are ascertained through the locally elected bodies concerned interacting with the local people[29].

In order to integrate various block level and district level projects with the State plan as a whole, they are first discussed with the State Planning board and thus total cohesion is ensured in the entire planning process in the State[30].

Summing Up

Though the concept of decentralised Planning (or grass-roots planning or Planning from below) has been accepted, still planning and decision-making function remained centralized at two levels—the Centre and the States. An appraisal of the progress towards decentralization of planning process in different states reveals a depressing picture. The style of planning in the states have been planning from the top and the people in general have no say or limited say in the planning process. While the developments in a few states, like Karnataka, West Bengal, Assam, Gujarat and Maharashtra, are noteworthy, the measures so far taken by the other States have not shown any significant or improvement on the planning process at the sub-State level. The slow progress is largely due to lack of political will and commitment to make the scheme of decentralised planning a success. In the absence of a clear directive from the political authority at the State level, the bureaucratic response to planning commission's persuasions and preaching on decentralised planning has been lukewarm. The failure is largely due to lack of political determination at the district level to assert their right priorities and for necessary financial autonomy for taking up the programmes best suited to the local needs. Failure in financial decentralisation is more glaring than in decentralisation of administration of economic programmes. The general hesitancy on the part of State bureaucracy for delegation of powers and functions to the local institutions has adversely affected the decentralisation of planning process in the States.

To sum up, the Indian experience with the decentralisation of planning process shows that much has been achieved but much more remains to be done. The need now is to recognise that the main objective of decentralisation of planning was to bring the planning process within the reach of the people. It is time that we went whole hog towards this goal. This may also prove to be in ultimate strength of the decentralized planning process.

REFERENCES

1. Government of Andhra Pradesh, Planning and Co-operation Department, *Fifth Five Year Plan, Draft Outline,* Regional Development, p. 535.
2. N. Somase Somasekhara, *States Planning in India: Technique, Procedures and Management, Vol. II, State Profiles,* Himalaya Publishing House, Delhi, 1985, pp. 17-18.
3. *Ibid.*, p. 18.
4. *Ibid.*, p. 18-19.
5. *Ibid.*, pp. 25-26.
6. Government of Andhra Pradesh, Abstract, G.O. Ms. No. 2, *Planning and Cooperation* (Plg. II), dated 1st Jan. 1972, p. 1.
7. N. Somasekhara, *op. cit.*, p. 26.
8. *Ibid.*, p. 26.
9. Sujit Sikidar, "Decentralised Planning Introduced in Assam", *Commerce,* Vol. 152, No. 3914, May 24, 1986, p. 1045.
10. *Ibid.*
11. *Ibid.*
12. *Ibid.*
13. *Ibid.*
14. *Ibid.*
15. *Ibid.*
16. *Ibid.*
17. *Ibid.*
18. N. Somasekhara, *op. cit.*, pp. 63-64.
19. Government of Gujarat, *Perspective Plan of Gujarat, 1974-1985,* vol. III, p. 136.
20. N. Somasekhara Khara, *op. cit.*, p. 108.
21. *Ibid.*
22. *Ibid.*, p. 109.
23. State Planning Commission, *'Perspective Plan for Tamil Nadu: 1974-84'*, 1974, p. 68.
24. P.C. Mahanti, "Decentralised Planning—West Bengal Starts the Process", *Commerce,* Vol. 152, No. 3914, May 24, 1986, p. 1021.
25. *Ibid.*

26. *Ibid.*
27. *Ibid.*
28. *Ibid.*
29. *Ibid.*
30. *Ibid.*, p. 1044.

7

Framework for Future

Today Planning in India is being done not only at the National and State levels but also at the district and local levels. The idea is that such a process would generate developmental impulses at all territorial levels. It would help to solve problems whenever they are; would mobilize resources whenever they can; and would involve people individually and in groups in developmental processes in each area and locality. In fact, planning is being done at a number of territorial levels. This decentralised planning system is vogue in India, suffer from almost the same deficiencies as the national planning system. It is technocratic in approach and lacks pcpular involvement. Its conceptual and theoretical foundations are weak and it is impregnated with a value system which is different from that of the people who are the main concern of development. In a multi-level planning set-up, the macro or micro issue is not simply an issue of scale, nor only an issue of resource allocation. It is not only the issue of decentralisation. It is an issue of a new way of looking at the developmental process—an issue of a new developmental style. It must be viewed as a two way process top down and bottom up simultaneously; it must be seen as the concern of the people; it must inform all aspects of life economic, social and cultural. If people's primary institution for collective action is the community, community participation i.e., role for ordinary people in matters affecting their lives, must become the cornerstone of planning.[1]

To overcome the problems of planning Dr. Deva Raj had suggested way back in 1973 to be the pre-conditions of multi-level planning. These are—*(a)* identification of levels of planning with territorial, spatial and administrative jurisdictions, *(b)* a hierarchy of levels inter-related to a hierarchy of functions, in matters of planning and implementations, *(c)* a system of inter-level or inter-governmental relationships—technical, financial and administrative—including arrangements for reviewing and determining policies, programmes and priorities as well as providing an integrated framework for local, State and National plans, *(d)* viability of local and the regional planning and executive units, agencies or level of Government for effective functioning and availability at each level of appropriate expertise for project formulation with necessary guidance and support from higher, echelons, and *(e)* a basic commitment to all out local planning and development effort with its attendant responsibilities of mobilization of local resources and exploitation of local potential with such outside support as may be necessary to induce self-generating growth.[2]

FAO has examined seven countries in the Asia and Pacific regions and stresses that the socio-political conditions and administrative structures of countries limits the extent to which planning can be decentralised in a particular country. The FAO volume has an interesting list of what may be called pre-requisites for multi-level planning efforts to be successfully experimented with: *(i)* political and official willingness and commitment to operate a multi-level planning system; *(ii)* an appropriate politico-administrative structure for multi-level planning clearly distinguishing the roles of the partners; *(iii)* a clear definition of function sharing among the levels; *(iv)* the provision of adequate financing to the various levels to match the functions to be performed in accordance with a rational allocation criteria; *(v)* the granting of the power and authority to mobilize funds at lower levels to augment transfers from higher levels; *(vi)* autonomy to plan for the decentralised sector in line with national priorities and objectives; *(vii)* a properly equipped planning machinery with adequate capabilities to plan, programme, analyse and translate projects; and *(viii)* adequate powers and authority at sub-national levels as well as freedom to function within reasonable limits of control.

The concept of decentralised planning incorporates the principles that proper decision-making is possible at any level if the strategy at each level is determined after a careful consideration of the potentials, needs and limitations of the next higher as well as the next lower level of planning. Thus, each level does not look upon planning as a self-contained activity at that territorial level, but recognizes the openness of the economy and always has an eye on spill over associations, inter-relationships and complementarities. Decentralised planning is a two way approach. It requires a lot of preparatory efforts from both ends. The higher level should give all macro framework indicators guidelines for planning. The lower level must feed the higher level with information and has also to prepare the plan from below. The two approaches will then have to be harmonized.

Area specific and people specific planning at the lowest level is decentralised or grass-root planning. The trigger potential in this type of planning is released by the people in the vital area of plan proposal initiation, processing and implementation. The social dynamics will play a vital role instead of bureaucracy and politics.

India lives in the villages. Gunnar Myrdal once said that there was only one economist who knew India that was Mahatma Gandhi. Here was a man who knew the power invested in rural communities and their problems. He wants to makes Indian village as republic. Thus, there is the need to plan at the grass-root level. According to 64th Constitutional Amendment, it has been envisaged to devolute powers to the Panchayats to draw up plans within the framework of guidelines and conditions to be stipulated by the State Government. It is further proposed that the major responsibility of the Panchayats will be implementation of development schemes as assigned to them by the State Government. It has been proposed to entrust the Panchayats with the responsibility for administration of poverty alleviation programmes, health and family welfare, women and child development, and the welfare programmes for all the weak and handicapped sections of rural society, the maintenance of community assets, etc. Under this changing political scenario in which there would be greater devolution of powers to the Panchayati Raj Institutions and associating them in the planning exercise, it is felt that planning machinery needs to be provided for, from the lowest rung onward.

The aim of such decentralised planning should be to provide for the basic amenities of life to the people, especially the disadvantaged sections of the society, increase productivity, provide gainful employment nearer to houses of the rural population, self-reliance, effective participation in decision making as well as plan implementation.

Keeping in mind the constitutional and politico-economic set up in the country, plans should be formulated and implemented at the national, state, district, block and village levels. No water-tight compartments should be drawn in this respect. If decentralised planning is to be successful in the true sense it is necessary to associate the PRIs with planning. At the most, we can suggest the areas/sectors which can be planning responsibilities of the various levels of planning hierarchy. The State within the framework of state list can take responsibility for planning for major projects according to the need of the State, i.e. irrigation projects, large scale industries, state and national highways, higher and professional/technical education, tourism etc. At the district level and below, the items of planning can be agriculture, horticulture, welfare of the backward classes, tribal, animal husbandry, community development, water supply and such projects/schemes which have local level implications. In other words *(a)* the plans that have intra state dimensions should be formulated at the national level, *(b)* plans having intra district dimensions should be formulated at the State level, *(c)* plans which have intra block dimensions should be formulated at district levels, and *(d)* plans which have intra Panchayats dimensions should be formulated at block level.

We may now indicate in detail the various procedures involved in decentralised planning. The first step in the decentralised planning process is the determination of appropriate levels of decision-making with reference to various activities. This would include *(i)* establishment of a suitable planning machinery or structure at that level which will be the nucleus planning body; *(ii)* defining the scope and functions of planning at each level; and *(iii)* deciding on inter area allocation of resources among different levels. The second step in the decentralised planning process involves organising interaction between different levels in terms of exchange of information and organising interactive consultations at different stages of plan formulation and plan appraisal. This step is the most important and the success of a decentralised planning operation would depend on the frequency and efficiency of this process of interaction. Suitable methodology will have to be evolved for this repetitive process to be successful. The third step in the decentralised planning process is what is called the 'vesting' (vesting implies securing both balances within the plans drawn up for different levels and also their harmonization) of plans at different levels and integrating them into a unified frame. Securing integration within plans at different level implies achieving balance at three level viz., sectoral, spatial and operational levels. At each level, the balance has to be achieved within certain parameters. Sectoral balance has to be achieved with due consideration for national and state priorities, local relevance, economic efficiency and internal consistency. In the same way, spatial balance has to be taken into account considerations like location, accessibility, network or international efficiency and threshold/viability/critical mass criteria, operational balance has to be achieved with due consideration to organisation, delegation of functions and powers, management procedures and personnel system. The integration of plans at various levels itself is a very complicated process. Therefore integrated plans of different levels will then have to be harmonized.

The trend towards decentralisation of planning is gathering momentum. Several states have already established some planning machinery at the district level with organisation, staff, power and funds to make them functional. A few states have also started experimenting with decentralising the planning process at the block/taluka level and arrangements vary from State to state. The following appear to be some important pre-requisitive for decentralised planning; *(a)* identification of levels and functions to be performed at each level; *(b)* establishment of planning machinery at each level with suitable trained staff; *(c)* indications of outlays that would be available for planning at each level; *(d)* delegation of power matching resource and responsibilities in consonance with tasks assigned; and *(e)* well-defined procedure and time frame for various stages of planning to be accomplished.

In the Indian context the decentralised planning framework could be envisaged as follows; central planning may confine itself to planning for strategic commodities and services needed for the country as a whole as well as for purposes of international transactions. It would also be concerned with the formulation and implementation of programmes affecting quality of life. State planning would be concerned with major sectors of activities, particularly agriculture and allied activities and infrastructural provision (which will include irrigation, power, roads, transport and provision of social services), and problems of urbanization and migration. District planning will confine itself to projects that may be located within a district and may include minor and medium irrigation schemes, small scale industries, agriculture and animal husbandry and provision of social services.

In the proposed model of decentralised planning, the National Development Council will be at the apex to approve plan objectives and strategies and to decide on important policies and procedures. The Planning Commission will come next and will be concerned with perspective plans, five year plans, and annual plans. It will also be concerned with spatial planning, resources and foreign aid, indicative plan for the private sector, central plan for strategic commodities and services, general co-ordination and direction of State plans, and evaluation and review of plan programmes. At the State level, such planning will be concerned with plan formulation for all sectors and implementation of plans, evaluation of programmes and feedback. State planning departments will also integrate the plans at the regional and district levels. Below the State level, there will be district planning bodies which will be concerned with district planning and implementation thereof, evaluation of programme and feedback operations. Below the district level, there will be

Figure 7.1
Organisational and Operational Framework of Decentralised Planning

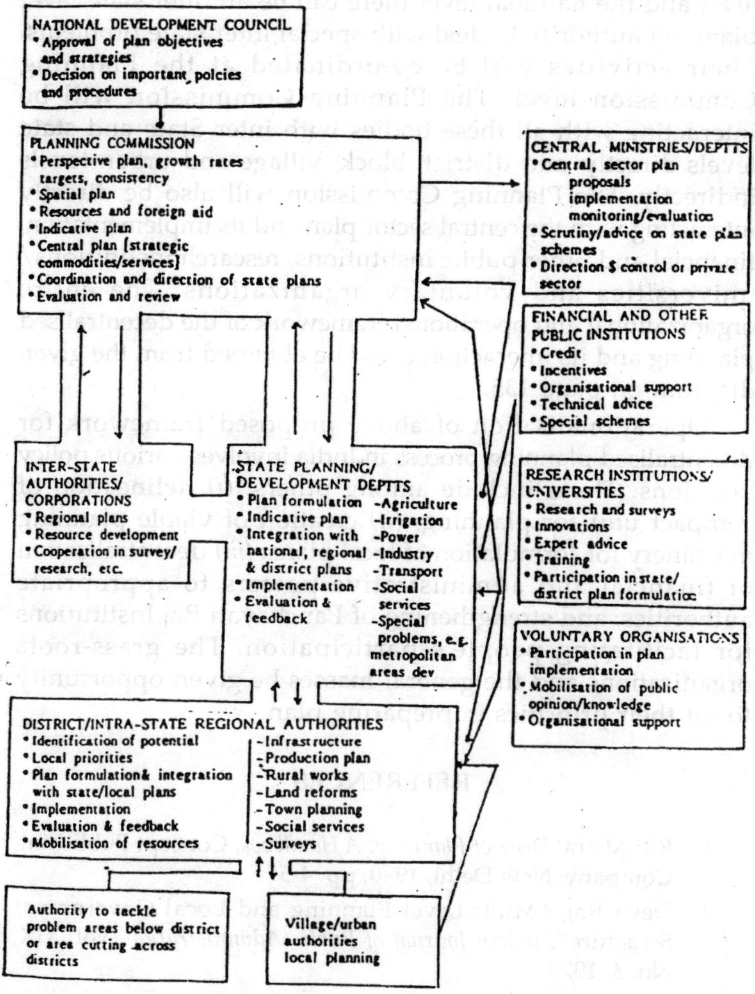

Source: R.P. Misra and K.V. Sundaram, *Multi-Level Planning and Integrated Rural Area Development*, Heritage Publishers, New Delhi 1978.

block level plans and village plans. The urban planning authorities will be separate from them. Also, sometimes, there may be regional planning for a group of districts which would be co-ordinated at the State level. Similarly, between the State level and the national level there can be an inter state level planning authority to deal with special inter state problems. Their activities will be co-ordinated at the Planning Commission level. The Planning Commission will be interacting with all these bodies with inter State and state levels directly, and district, block, village and urban levels indirectly. The Planning Commission will also be directly interacting with the central sector plan and its implementation, financial and other public institutions, research institutions/ universities and voluntary organizations. The entire organizational and operational framework of the decentralised planning and its interaction could be obtained from the given diagram on page 135.

Operationalisation of above proposed framework for decentralised planning process in India involves various policy decisions. These include among others: *(i)* delineation of compact unit for planning; *(ii)* creation of viable planning machinery for formulation of local plans; *(iii)* decentralisation of financial and administrative powers to appropriate authorities; and strengthening of Panchayati Raj Institutions for facilitating people's participation. The grass-roots organisations and the general masses be given opportunity to set their priorities in preparing plan.

REFERENCES

1. R.P. Misra, *District Planning: A Handbook*, Concept Publishing Company, New Delhi, 1990, pp. 4-5.
2. Deva Raj, "Multi-Level Planning and Local Government Structure", *Indian Journal of Public Administration*, Vol. XIX, No. 3, 1973.

8

Summary and Suggestions

There is now an increasing realization of the need for decentralised planning for a country like India. The issues are how much to decentralise and how to operationalise it. The forty-five years of centralised planning has failed to fulfil the objective of planning.

The issue in decentralised planning, therefore, that are of major concern has moved away considerably over the past two decades. Though real India resides in villages yet planning for them is done from Delhi or State Capitals. The Central/State Government is a remote authority to an ordinary villagers. But the village Panchayats are directly elected by the villagers, and these elected members are their neighbour. So the programmes undertaken at the Gram Panchayat level are of direct relevance and of direct interest to the villagers. And when local plans are expounded, discussed and approved at the local level, the villager becomes a participant in the process of plan formulation. Only in this manner can people be enthused to plan for their own future development and to participate in the plan exercise. The participation and involvement of the common people in the planning process require that a part of the decision-making process should be left to the people themselves. They must decide on the priorities of development in terms of their own perceptions of needs and priorities.

The subject of decentralised planning or grass-root planning or planning from below has been engaging the serious attention of the planners and policy makers ever since the inception of the First Five Year Plan. But the experience of decentralisation of the planning process reveal that very little had been achieved and much more remains to be done. The need now is to recognise that the main objective of decentralization was to bring the planning process within reach of the people.

The present system of decentralised planning and its method of resource allocation and decision-making looks at the people and their problems from above and suffers from the same deficiencies as the national macro-planning system, with its technocratic approach and with Central and State agencies going right down to the district and even the village level. As the existing socio-political structure and Panchayati Raj bodies are dominated by vested interests, it is necessary, to involve the Gram Sabha (the total assembly of the village people), cooperative societies and other local institutions, to ensure that the fruits of development must reach the people. Therefore, decentralised planning has to go far below the district level and the focus should be on the people. The plans for the district should be simple, so that the people, who participate in framing those plans, can understand their scope, limitations and content.

In the present system of planning, bureaucracy escaped accountability, whereas if power is given to the Panchayati Raj Institutions, they would be accountable to the people, forcing them to prepare a more people-oriented plan.

In fact, decentralisation of planning system must not be a gift to the PRIs; but a matter of right for them. The political set-up should have the will to give up its power. Because, decentralisation actually involves people at village and at panchayat levels. There is a need for the popularization of the concept of decentralisation in planning. The fundamental to the driving forces for decentralised planning is the behaviour of ordinary people, their needs, their aspirations and other overriding ideas. The local Governments have to think and act both globally and nationally but serve the people locally, taking on socio-economic responsibilities from the national Government.

The three high powered committees set up to report on this issue of decentralisation are: (i) National Committee on Panchayati Raj Institutions, 1978; (ii) Working Group on Block Level Planning, 1978; (iii) Working Group on District Planning, 1984; under the chairmanship of Ashoka Mehta, M.L. Dantwala and C.H. Hanumantha Rao respectively. Despite these steps, D.T. Lakdawala, former Deputy Chairman of the Planning Commission assessed the position in 1984 as follows: "while decentralised planning has been talked of for a long time and the first guide lines for the formulation of district planning were laid down as early as in 1969, the activity has remained a 'non-starer' is still valid.

It has been pointed out by many scholars that decentralised planning needs a number of essential preconditions which are still lacking. These include statutory measures to create sub-state-level Governments with adequate devolution of resources and decision-making powers, political mobilization of the weak and the disadvantaged in the rural areas to countervail the likely growing power of the local rural elite in the wake of coming into being of new tier of Government at the district and lower levels and progress towards building up administrative personnel at these levels capable of achieving intersectoral coordination and willing to work under the guidance of local-level political leaders. It is indeed ture that genuine and effective decentralised planning would remain beyond our reach unless these pre-conditions are achieved in a substantial measure.

The operational effectiveness of decentralised planning depend in the long run on the soundness of its economic perspective, of objectives and criteria guiding it and of information system for feedback and horning borning.

Beyond the initial phase, the effectiveness of decentralised planning system would depend on two types of political processes: *(a)* mobilization of rural elite and middle strata, which is already evident in a number of States, to get more development resources and attention for rural areas, and *(b)* mobilisation of rural poor, which in scale and intensity is still very modest, to put pressure on both Government and rural elite for a larger developmental share for the poor. Generally both the official agencies and the rural activists tend to neglect this point.

Decentralised planning in India suffer from certain impediments which make it rather impossible to achieve the objective. Decentralised planning is not supposed to work in vacuum. For its success, effective institutions of basic democracy are required. Here Panchayati Raj Institutions could have played a constructive role.

Everything said and done, the fact remains that though decentralised planning process remains a laudable goal in the era of Indian planning, the facts on the ground do not call for any shift to decentralisation. Much ground work has to be done before embarking on any ambitious scheme of decentralised planning.

Decentralised planning means that there are local decision-making agencies have more or less independent existence and power. Under the existing set up in India, the decisions are taken by a few at the top, and quite naturally they go in favour of the few.

SUGGESTIONS

In order to make decentralised planning effective, few suggestions are mentioned below:—

Political Aspects

(a) On the political front there should be greater devolution of power to the lower levels of political power hierarchy.

(b) Local institutions like Panchayati Raj Institutions should be strengthened.

(c) Regular elections to the local bodies/institutions should be held and ensured by constitutional amendment.

(d) The development schemes along with necessary finances should be provided to local bodies.

(e) Delineation of compact unit for planning.

(f) Creation of viable planning machinery for formulation of local plans.

(g) A genuine political commitment in favour of decentralisation of planning is must.

Administrative Aspects

(a) The specialists should be accorded proper authority and final say on all technical matters.

(b) To augment the planning skills, it is suggested that the Planning Commission should be entrusted with the task of organising training courses for the State Planning officials as well as for the district planning. Key personal at regular intervals and it should be made a permanent feature of the planning commission. Similarly training by the State should be also made compulsory to all persons engaged in planning process so that all levels of personnels engaged in planning work possess the required planning skill and expertise.

(c) Evaluation and monitoring would be entrusted to an outside independent agency.

(d) To ensure proper co-ordination, it is suggested that at the State level a senior officer be appointed who would work in close association with the District Planning authority. Similarly at the district level a officer be appointed who would work in close association with the block and village level.

(e) Provision should be made for a regular flow of reliable, relevant data and a proper synchronisation of information system with the decision-making aspects of planning.

(f) A functionary should be posted for a fairly enough time so as to grasp the local problems. There should not be frequent transfer.

(g) There is also the need for a re-organisation of the district administration in tune with the district and block planning.

Financial Aspects

(a) Decentralisation of financial powers to appropriate authorities.

(b) It is suggested that the recommendation of the Sarkaria Commission regarding setting up of State Planning and Finance Board needs active consideration and implementation.

(c) It is necessary that there should be adequate and genuine devolution of financial powers to the district and block planning body.

Organisational Aspects

(a) At State, District, Block and Village level planning organisation should be created.

(b) District should be the nucleus of planning machinery and the following units should be created at the State level could be replicated at the district level, *(i)* Perspective Planning Unit, *(ii)* Plan formulation, monitoring and evaluation unit, *(iii)* Projects Formulation Unit; and *(iv)* Plan Coordination Unit.

Social Aspects

(a) Planning Body should be made as broad as is feasible.

(b) People's participation in the planning should be encouraged.

(c) People representing varied interests, classes, areas should be associated and the plans should be formed on the basis of local needs and with full knowledge of the socio-economic-cultural and of the people for whom the plan is meant.

(d) Voluntary and non-government organisation should be actively associated with the development plans.

(e) Pressure groups representing the economic/social/cultural aspects should be encouraged to be established.

To sum up it may be said that decentralised planning is not as simple as it looks. Capabilities have to be built up, suitable structures have to be evolved, changes have to be brought about in the administrative, political as well as operational level. Equally important is kindling the zeal and enthusiasm of the people. But the most important agents to make decentralised planning a success in real sense, is the political and administrative will to decentralise powers to the lower levels. With a clear policy enunciation, full political support, and needed administrative infrastructure, it is expected that the goals of decentralised planning will be achieved.

Bibliography

PRIMARY SOURCES

Public Documents

Government of India, First Five Year Plan, Planning Commission, New Delhi, 1951.

Government of India, Second Five Year Plan, Planning Commission, New Delhi, 1956.

Government of India, Report of the Committee on Plan Projects, Planning Commission, New Delhi, 1957.

Government of India, Third Five Year Plan, Planning Commission, New Delhi, 1961.

Government of India, Final Report of the Study Team on the Machinery of Planning, Administrative Reforms Commission, New Delhi, 1967.

Government of India, Fourth Five Year Plan, Planning Commission, New Delhi, 1969a.

Government of India, Guidelines for the Formulation of District Plans, Planning Commission, New Delhi, 1969b.

Government of India, Fifth Five Year Plan, Planning Commission, New Delhi, 1974.

Government of India, Report of the Working Group on Block Level Planning, Planning Commission, New Delhi, 1978a.

Government of India, Report of the Committee on Panchayati Raj Institutions, Department of Rural Development, Ministry of Agriculture and Irrigation, New Delhi, 1978b.

Government of India, Sixth Five Year Plan, Planning Commission, New Delhi, 1980.

Government of India, Report of the Working Group on District Planning, Planning Commission, New Delhi, 1984.

Government of India, Seventh Five Year Plan, Planning Commission, 1985a.

Government of India, Report of the Committee to Review the Existing Administrative Arrangements for Rural Development, Ministry of Rural Development, New Delhi, 1985b.

Government of India, Towards Improved Local Level Planning for Rural Development: Lessons from Experience, Planning Commission, New Delhi, 1986.

Government of India, The Report of the Commission on Centre-State Relations, Part I and II, Government of India, New Delhi, 1988.

Government of India, Report of the Study Group on Training for District Planning, Planning Commission, New Delhi, 1985a.

Government of India, Report of the Committee of the Study Group on Information Gap, Planning Commission, New Delhi, 1985b.

Government of Uttar Pradesh, Decentralised Planning, Draft Annual Plan, Vol. I, Review 1984-85, State Planning Department, 1983.

SECONDARY SOURCES

Books

Adiseshiah, Malcolm S., et. al., *Decentralised Planning and Panchayati Raj: Proceedings of the D.T. Lakdawala Memorial Symposium*, Institute of Social Sciences, New Delhi, 1994.

Agarwal, A.N., and Kundan Lal, *Economic Planning: Principles, Techniques and Practice,* 2nd ed., Vikas, New Delhi, 1980.

Ahuja, Kanta (ed.), *District Planning in Rajasthan,* The HCM State Institute of Public Administration, Jaipur, 1977.

Awasthi, D.S., *Decentralised Planning in India,* The Indian Economic Association, Kanpur, 1990.

Baisya, K.N. and D.D. Mali, *Decentralised Planning,* Metropolitan Book Co., New Delhi, 1989.

Balkrishna, R., *Regional Planning in India,* Bangalore Printing and Publishing Co., Bangalore, 1948.

Banerji, Mrityunjoy, *Planning in India,* Oxford and IBH, New Delhi, 1981.

Battelheim, Charles, *Some Basic Planning Problems,* Asia, Bombay, 1961.

Bhattacharya, K.N., *Indian Plans: A Generalist Approach,* Asia Publishing House, Calcutta, 1963.

Blitzer Charles R., *Economy Wise Models and Development Planning,* Oxford University Press, London, 1977.

Chansarkar, B.A., *Models for Planning in India,* Himalaya Publishing House, Bombay, 1983.

Chakravarty, Sukhamoy, *Capital and Development Planning,* M.I.T. Press, Cambridge, 1969.

Desai, P.B., *Planning in India,* Vikas, Ghaziabad, 1979.

Dhar, D.P., *Planning and Social Change,* Arnold-Heinmann, New Delhi, 1976.

Dobb, Maurice, *Some Aspects of Economic Development,* University of Delhi, Delhi, 1951.

Dubhashi, P.R, *Grammer of Planning: Concepts and Applications,* IIPA, New Delhi, 1983.

Gadgil, D.R., *Planning and Economic Policy in India,* Asia Publishing House, Poona, 1965.

Gedam, Ratnakar, *Development Planning: Origin and Growth,* Akashdeep Publishing House, New Delhi, 1991.

Ghosh, Arun, *Planning in India: The Challenge for the Nineties*, Sage Publications, New Delhi, 1992.

Gupta, Ranjit, *Prelude to Block Level Planning in Gujarat*, Indian Institute of Management, Ahmedabad, 1978.

Hilhorst, J.G.M., *Regional Planning: A Systems Approach*, Rotterdam University Press, Rotterdam, 1971.

Hooja, Rakesh and P.C. Mathur, *District and Decentralized Planning*, Rawat, Jaipur, 1991.

I.C.C.S.R., *Survey of Research in India*, Popular Prakashan, Bombay, 1972.

Inamdar, N.R. and V.K. Kshire, *District Planning in India: A Case Study of Maharashtra*, Oxford and IBH Publishing Co., New Delhi, 1986.

Jain, Anil Kumar, *Economic Planning in India*, Ashish Publishing House, New Delhi, 1986.

Kabra, K.N., *Planning Process in a District*, IIPA, New Delhi, 1977.

Koontz, Harold and Cyril O. Donnell, *Essentials of Management*, Tata McGraw Hill Publishing Co., New Delhi, 1980.

Krishnamachari, V.T., *Fundamentals of Planning in India*, Orient Longmans, Bombay, 1962.

Kumar, Birendra, *An Introduction to Planning in India*, Bookland, Calcutta, 1962.

Kumarappa, J.C., *Planning by the People for the People*, Vora, Bombay, 1954.

Lewis, Arthur W., *Development Planning: The Essentials of Economic Policy*, George Allen and Unwin, London, 1966.

Marx, F. Moretein, *Elements of Public Administration*, PHI, New Delhi, 1968.

Marx, K. and F. Engels, *Manifesto of the Communist Party*, Masco, 1953.

Mehta, Ashok, *The Plan: Perspective and Problems*, Bharatiya Vidya Bhavan, Bombay, 1966.

Mehta, Ashok, *Economic Planning in India*, Young Indian Publications, New Delhi, 1970.

Mishra, Baidyanath, *Capitalism, Socialism and Planning*, Oxford and IBH Publishing Co., New Delhi, 1972.

Mishra, Sweta, *Democratic Decentralisation in India*, Mittal Publications, New Delhi, 1994.

Mishra, Sweta, *Changing Pattern of District Administration*, Mittal Publications, New Delhi, 1996.

Mishra, S.N., *Decentralisation in Development*, Mittal Publications, New Delhi, 1991.

Mishra, S.N., *Participative Management and Rural Development*, Mittal Publications, New Delhi, 1992.

Mishra, S.N., *Rural Development and Panchayati Raj*, Concept, New Delhi, 1981.

Mishra, S.N. and S.S. Singh, *Roads to Model Panchayati Raj*, Mittal Publications, New Delhi, 1993.

Mishra, S.N., *New Horizons in Rural Development Administration*, Mittal Publications, New Delhi, 1989.

Misra, R.P., D.V. Urs and V.K. Natraj (eds.), *Regional Planning and National Development*, Vikas, New Delhi, 1978.

Misra, R.P. (ed.), *Local-level Planning and Development*, Sterling, New Delhi, 1983.

Misra, R.P., *District Planning: A Handbook*, Concept, New Delhi, 1990.

Misra, R.P., V.L.S. Parkasa Rao and K.V. Sundaram (eds.), *Regional Development Planning in India: A New Strategy*, Vikas, New Delhi, 1974.

Misra, R.P. and K.V. Sundaram (eds.), *Multi-level Planning and Integrated Rural Development in India*, Heritage Publications, New Delhi, 1979.

Mosher, Frederick, C., *Program Budgeting*, Public Administration Service, Chicago, 1954.

Myrdal, Gunnar, *Asian Drama: An Inquiry Into Poverty of Nations*, The Penguin Press, London, 1968.

Nandwani, S.C., *Planning and Development in India*, Cosmopolitan Publishing House, Phagwara, 1965.

Natraj, Lalitha, *An Analysis into the Political Aspects of Planning in India (with special reference to Karnataka)*, Inter-India Publications, New Delhi, 1985.

Natraj, V.K., *Decentralisation of Planning in India*, Institute of Development Studies, Mysore, 1974.

Nayar, P.K.B., *Leadership Bureaucracy and Planning in India: A Sociological Study*, Associated Publishing House, New Delhi, 1969.

Panjabi, Kewal, *The Civil Servant in India*, Bharatiya Vidya Bhavan, Bombay, 1965.

Parmar, Mary, *Development Planning in India*, Reliance Publishing House, New Delhi, 1992.

Paranjape, H.K., *The Planning Commission: A Descriptive Study*, IIPA, New Delhi, 1964.

Patankar, Mamatha, *Economic Planning*, Sultan Chand and Sons, New Delhi, 1977.

Patil, V.G., *An Analysis of Plan Implementation in India*, Balgovind Prakashan, Ahmedabad, 1969.

Prasad, Kamta, *Planning at the Grass Roots*, Sterling Publishers, New Delhi, 1988.

Rao, V.K.R.V., *Planning Unit Areas for Integrated Rural Development—An Exercise*, Ashish Publishing House, New Delhi, 1980.

Raza, Moonis, *Regional Development*, Heritage Publishers, New Delhi, 1988.

Reddy, Y. Venugopal, *Multilevel Planning in India*, Vikas, New Delhi, 1979.

Roy, Ajit, *Planning in India: Achievements and Problems*, National Publishers, Calcutta, 1965.

Ruddar Datt and K.P.M. Sundaram (ed.), *Indian Economy*, S. Chand and Co., New Delhi, 1973.

Santhanam, K., *Democratic Planning: Problems and Pitfals*, Asia, Bombay, 1961.

Sen, Lalit K., *Readings in Micro-Level Planning and Rural Growth Centres*, National Institute of Community Development, Hyderabad, 1973.

Sharma, R.D., *District Administration in India: Problems and Prospects*, H.K. Publishers, New Delhi, 1990.

Sinha, R.K., *Economic Planning in India*, Deep and Deep Publications, New Delhi, 1986.

Sinha, U.M., *Personal Administration, Concept and Comparative Perspective*, R.B.S.A. Publishers, Jaipur, 1986.

Somasekhara, N., *State's Planning in India*, Himalaya Publishing House, Delhi, 1985.

Tandon, B.C., *Economic Planning: Theory and Practice*, Chaitanya Publishing House, Allahabad, 1970.

Thakur, Devendra and S.N. Singh, *District Planning and Panchayati Raj*, Deep and Deep Publications, New Delhi, 1991.

United Nations, *A Handbook of Public Administration*, New York, 1961.

United Nations, *Government Budgeting and Economic Planning in Developing Countries*, New York, 1966.

Urwick, L., *The Elements of Administration*, Harper and Brothers, New York, 1943.

Vakil, C.N. and Brahmananda, *Planning for a Shortage Economy*, Vora and Co., Bombay, 1952.

Vishveswaraya, M., *District Development Scheme—Economic Progress by Forced Marches*, Bangalore Press, Bangalore, 1942.

Vyas, V.S., Anil Bhatt and A.M. Shah, *Decentralised Planning in India*, Oxford and IBH, Delhi, 1985.

Yugandhar, B.N. and Amitava Mukherjee, *Foundations of Decentralisation*, Heritage Publishers, New Delhi, 1990.

Yugandhar, B.N. and Amitava Mukherjee, *Researches in Decentralisation*, Heritage Publishers, New Delhi, 1990.

Yugandhar, B.N. and Amitava Mukherjee, *Methodology and Database for Decentralised Planning*, Heritage Publishers, New Delhi, 1991.

Yugandhar, B.N. and Amitava Mukherjee, *Readings in Decentralised Planning*, Concept, New Delhi, 1991.

Articles

Anand, Swarup, "District Planning", *Journal of the National Academy of Administration* (Mussoorie), Vol. 15, No. 4, October-December 1970.

Adiseshiah, Malcolm S., "Decentralised Planning and Cooperative Federalism", *Mainstream,* Vol. 30, No. 50, 3 October 1992.

Arora, Hari C., "Decentralised Planning", *Indian Journal of Public Administration,* Vol. 37, No. 2, April-June 1991.

Binniger, Aneeta, "Rural Development and Decentralised Planning: Who should Participate and How?", *The Administrator,* Vol. 36, No. 3, July-September 1991.

Bhargava, Gopal, "District Planning and National Development", *Society and Commerce,* Vol. 3, No. 9, December 1974.

Bhargava, Gopal, "Towards District Level Planning", *Young India,* 12 July 1973.

Bhagi, P.N., "Block-Level Planning", *Economic Times,* 24 September 1979.

Datta, Chaudhari Mrinal, "New Delhi Government Committed to Decentralisation", *Economic Times,* December 13th, 1989.

Deva Raj, "Multi-Level Planning and Local Government Structure", *Indian Journal of Public Administration,* Vol. 19, No. 3, July-September 1973.

Dubhashi, P.R., "Decentralization, Planning and Public Administration", *Indian Journal of Public Administration,* Vol. 12, No. 1, January-March 1966.

Dutta, Vijay Ranjan, "Planning from below: A New Role of Panchayati Raj Institutions", *Khadi Gramodyog,* Vol. 14, No. 11, August 1968.

Economic Advisory Council, "First Report of Decentralisation of Development and Implementation in the State", *Economic Times,* January 14th, 1984.

Fischer, Benjamin H., "Growth Centre Planning in India" in R.P. Mishra and K.V. Sundaram, (eds.) *Rural Area Development and Approaches,* Sterling Publishers, Delhi, 1979.

Ghosh, Arun, "Decentralised Planning: West Bengal Experience", *Economic and Political Weekly,* Vol. XXII, No. 13, March 26th, 1988.

Gulati, I.S., "Decentralised Planning: Loopholes that Remain", *Economic and Political Weekly,* Vol. XXI, No. 32, August 9, 1986.

Handa, K.L., "Planning and Budgeting in India: Concept and Practice", *Indian Journal of Public Administration,* Vol. 30, No. 3, July-September 1984.

Jain, R.B., "Planning in the Third World: An Overview of Experiences in India", *Indian Journal of Public Administration,* Vol. XXX, No. 3, July-September 1984.

Kabra, Kamal Nayan, "Centre-State Relations and Purposive Decentralised Planning", *Mainstream,* Vol. 27, No. 40, July 1989.

Khatu, K.K., "Rural Planning System", *The National Geographical Journal of India,* Vol. XXI, Pts. 3 and 4, 1975.

Kunwar, Upendra, "Decentralised Planning in India", *Khadi Gramodyog,* Vol. 35, No. 11, August 1989.

Minocha, A.C., "Planning for Social Services in a Backward Region", *Indian Journal of Regional Science,* Vol. VI, No. 2, 1974.

Mishra, S.N. and Sweta Mishra, "Political Process and Political Parties in India: Retrospect and Prospect", *Indian Journal of Public Administration,* 1994.

Mishra, S.N. and Sweta Mishra, "Future of Panchayati Raj After 73rd Constitutional Amendment Act", *Kurukshetra,* Vol. XLIII, No. 7, April 1995.

Misra, R.P. and M. Shivalingaih, "Growth Pole Strategy for Development in India", *Journal of the Institute of Economic Geography,* Vol. 1, 1970.

Mohanti, P.C., "Decentralised Planning—West Bengal Starts the Process", *Commerce,* Vol. 152(3914), May 24, 1986.

Prasad, C.S., "District Planning: An Approach to Decentralised Planning", *The Administrator,* Vol. 36, July-September 1991.

Prasad, Kamta, "Integrated Framework for Decentralised Planning—Issues and Option", *Gandhian Perspective*, Vol. V, No. 2, 1992.

Sen, Lalit K., "The Growth Centre and its Application to Development Planning", *Administrative Staff College of India Journal of Management*, 1971.

Singh, Ajit Kumar, "Decentralised Planning under Five Year Plans: Emerging Perspectives", *Space*, Vol. 4, No. 3, July 1989.

Singh, V.S., "Decentralised Planning Needs Reorientation", *Yojana*, July 1-15, 1987.

Sisodia, H.G.S., "Graft Hits Plan for Rural Poor", *The Hindustan Times*, October 11th, 1983.

Srivastava, K.B., "Management of Rural Development in India: The Case of Decentralised Planning", *Journal of Rural Development*, Vol. 9, No. 2, March 1990.

Thaha, M., "Decentralised Planning for Rural Infrastructure", *The Administrator*, Vol. 36, No. 3, July-September 1991.

Thapliyal, B.K., "Decentralised Planning: Concept, Scope and Methodology", *Journal of Rural Development*, Vol. 9(6), 1990.

Thavaraj, M.J.K., "Politics of Planning", *Indian Journal of Public Administration*, Vol. 30, No. 3, July-September, 1994.

APPENDIX-I

DECENTRALISED PLANNING RATIONALE

1. FAILURES OF CENTRALISED PLANNING.
2. DIVERSITIES, DETAILS AND INFORMATION COSTS.
3. COORDINATED VS UNCOORDINATED DEPARTMENTAL EFFORTS.
4. SOCIO-POLITICAL GOAL: PEOPLE'S PARTICIPATION, etc.

DECENTRALISED PLANNING MACHINERY

(DISTRICT LEVEL)

AUTHORITY	**CDP**	**TECHNICAL**
ZILA PARISHAD	—BRMC 1957	— Dist Stat. Off.
DISTRICT PLAN COMMUNITY	—ARC	— Dist. Plan Off.
	—PLAN. COMM. GUIDELINES 1969	— (Stress on Process)
ZILA PARISHAD	—DANTWALA —(A. MEHTA)	— DIST. PLANNING CELL Chief Plan Off. + 6 Technical Off.
	—1982 GUIDELINES	— -do- (+ fin. assist)
DISTRICT PLAN BODY/ STEERING COMMITTEE	-- RAO COMMITTEE	— Status of Plan Off. & Cell

Source: Pranab Banerjee, District Planning, in S.N. Mishra, Course Material of Fifth Training of Trainers Programme on New Panchayati Raj (Nov. 27-Dec. 9, 1995).

DECENTRALISED PLANNING MACHINERY

(BLOCK LEVEL)

AUTHORITY			TECHNICAL
	CDP		EDO + Eos (VLW + PEOPLE
PANCHYAT SAMITI	— BRMC		
	— DANTWALA	—	'PERPATETIC' DIST. TEAM
MANDAL	— S MEHTA	—	
	— C.H.H. RAO	—	DIST. LEVEL + PLANNING OFF + 2 RAs (Single Planning Cadre)

LESSONS FROM THE PAST

1. LACK OF UNDERSTANDING AND SKILLS FOR DECENTRALISED PLANNING
2. ROLE OF BUREAUCRACY
3. INADEQUATE DEVOLUTION OF FINANCIAL POWERS
4. SUBORDINATE STATUS OF PRIs & ROLE OF POLITICIANS
5. NATIONAL IMPERATIVES.

PREREQUISITES OF DECENTRALISED PLANNING

1. CLARITY OF SCOPE & CONTENT
2. FINANCIAL DEVOLUTION

3. SUITABLE DISTRICT/BLOCK PLANNING AUTHORITIES
4. TECHNICAL PLANNING MACHINERY AND WELL-TRAINED MOTIVATED PERSONNEL
5. SUITABLE ADMINISTRATIVE REORGANISATION SPECIALLY FOR IMPLEMENTATION
6. PEOPLE'S INVOLVEMENT

HOW TO PLAN

1. **BROAD OBJECTIVES AND CONCRETE TARGETS**
   AGGREGATE
   SECTORAL
   CLASS-WISE
2. **BUILDING DATA BASE**
   RESOURCES
   DEMOGRAPHIC
   SOCIO-ECONOMIC
   INFRASTRUCTURE
   AGRO-ECONOMIC
   SECTORAL
   SPECIAL PROBLEMS OF AVAILABILITY OF DISAGGREGATED DATA QUESTION OF TECHNIQUES
3. **MARRYING (1) & (2) TO PREPARE DISTRICT PLAN**
   — HIGHLIGHTING MAJOR FEATURES
   — FORECASTING/ANTICIPATING PROBLEMS & OPPORTUNITIES
   DATA ANALYSES TECHNIQUES
   AND MOULDING DATA INTO CONCEPTUAL CATEGORIES
4. **FORMULATION PLAN STRATEGY**
   ECONOMICS, SPATIAL & MANPOWER PLANNING, POLICY ANALYSIS TOOLS

5. **TRANSLATION OF STRATEGY INTO SPECIFIC PROGRAMMES/PROJECTS/SCHEMES**
   - EXAMINE ONGOING PROJECTS/ PROGRAMMES: MODIFICATIONS, IMPROVEMENTS, LINKAGES
   - SHELF OF NEW PROJECTS/PROGRAMMES & THEIR PRIORITISATION: SEE LINKAGES, EMPLOYMENT POTENTIAL, GROWTH POTENTIAL, COST EFFECTIVENESS, LOCATION

TECHNIQUES OF PROJECT APPRAISAL GUIDELINES OF RAO COMMITTEE

ANNEX 6.5

SPATIAL & MANPOWER PLANNING TECHNIQUES
BASIC CONCEPTS OF INTER-SECTORAL LINKAGES

6. **ASSESSMENT OF RESOURCES**
   - RESOURCES FROM STATE PLAN
   - UNITED RESOURCES
   - LOCAL RESOURCE GENERATION
   - RESOURCES OF FINANCIAL INSTITUTIONS

   INPUTS FROM BUDGET/PLAN EXERCISES & CREDIT PLANS SIMPLE PROJECTION TECHNIQUES

7. **DRAWING UP THE PLAN**

PEOPLE'S NEEDS	RESOURCE & DEV. BASE
TECHNICAL EXPERTISE	FINANCIAL RESOURCES

   (LINKAGES, COST EFFECTIVENESS, GROWTH POTENTIAL, EQUITY, EMPLOYMENT & SPATIAL CONSIDERATIONS)

8. **IMPLEMENTATION**
   - CO-ORDINATION ETC.
   - FLEXIBILITY

9. **MONITORING AND EVALUATION**

PROJECT FORMULATION GUIDELINES (ANNEX 6.5 RAO COMMITTEE)

I. EMPLOYMENT GENERATION IN EXISTING OCCUPATIONS.

II. COMPLEMENTARY AND SUPPLEMENTARY INVESTMENTS.

III. PRODUCTIVE USE OF LOCAL NEGLECTED RESOURCES.

IV. BENEFICIARY GROUP ORIENTED INVESTMENTS.

V. LOCATION WITH RESPECT TO LABOUR.

VI. LEAD SECTOR & PACKAGE APPROACH TOWARDS NEW SCHEMES.

VII. BASIC NEEDS.

VIII. COORDINATION WITH ONGOING & COMPLETED PROJECTS.

IX. SIMPLE, SMALL & LOCAL.

(A) DESCRIPTION OF SCHEME & ITS LOCAL SIGNIFICANCE

(B) ITS LOCATION

(C) AMOUNTS & SOURCES OF INPUTS

(D) VOLUME & VALUE OF OUTPUT

(E) NUMBER OF BENEFICIARIES

(F) VOLUME OF EMPLOYMENT

APPENDIX-II

CHAPTER 4

DECENTRALISED PLANNING AT DISTRICT LEVEL AND BELOW*

4.1 The Seventh Plan lays considerable emphasis on decentralised planning. It is but natural that a subject like decentralised planning raises a host of issues and problems on the mechanics, dynamics and management of planning functions. This chapter is devoted to a discussion of these issues and problems. This discussion is quite relevant because the decentralisation effort is essentially a managerial activity which calls for a range of administrative or organizational devices that will improve the efficiency, effectiveness and responsiveness of planning at various levels.

4.2 In the history of planned development in our country, the Fourth Plan period (1969-74) stands out as a significant milestone. During this period, certain important departures both in the planning process as well as in the content of planning were introduced. The most important change was that in relation to the pattern of devolution of plan funds to the State level. This initiated a first stage of decentralisation of the planning process from the National to the State level in a realistic sense. Since then, the State Governments in the country have been building up their own machinery for planning at the State level and improving their planning methodologies. It may now be stated that planning as a technical activity at the level of the States has been firmly

---

Source: CAARD Report.

entrenched. The next step is to take this decentralisation process further down to the next appropriate level below the State. There is now broad consensus among experts, policy makers and planners that the basic unit for policy planning, project formulation and implementation at the sub-State level would be the district.

4.3 The concept of decentralised planning to the District level has been in the air for nearly three decades. The Community Development Programme launched by the Union Government in 1953 was motivated by the desire for decentralised development. In 1954, the State were asked to prepare District and Village Plans. In the late 50s', the Panchayati Raj Institutions were established at the district and lower levels to provide an institutional base for people's active involvement in development. A number of committees have subsequently been set up by the Government of India to examine the various issues connected with grassroots level planning and implementation. Special mention may be made in this context to the Dantwala Working Group on Block level planning, the Ashoka Mehta Committee on Panchayati Raj Institutions and the Planning Commission's Working Group on District Planning. We have carefully considered the various recommendations of these groups before setting out our views on the design of an appropriate organizational structure for planning and plan implementation at the district level.

4.4 The Working Group on District Planning has rightly emphasised that District Planning should be conceived as a single wholistic operation (and not as a fragmented operation (and not as a fragmented operation among many agencies) in which all individual sectoral programmes and projects would be harmonised into a unified planning activity. With such a concept of District Planning as the background, the Working Group has detailed the various arrangements necessary for rendering the district planning process effective, including the various pre-requisites that should be met, the institutional arrangements that should be devised and the essentials of a planning methodology that should be followed.

4.5 It has been noted that the States differ widely in their experience relating to decentralised district planning. For some States, the experience has been quite limited being confined at best only to one or two years. Consequently, the decentralisation procedures and methodologies are still evolving in these States. Most of the States are just launching some moves towards decentralisation of the planning process at the district level, some have moved a little afar, having devised certain measures of decentralisation (partial decentralisation). In fact, it is only a few States in the country like Maharashtra, Gujarat, Jammu & Kashmir, Uttar Pradesh, Karnataka and lately West Bengal which have mad some progress in this direction. But even in these States, the Working Group had observed that "real planning functions have not percolatated to the district level, nor the Panchayati Raj Institutions have been involved in the process". In Maharashtra, the Planning functions was initially entrusted to Panchayati Raj Institutions. But later, new District Planning bodies headed by the Minister of State have been set up. Similar set-ups have also emerged in Gujarat and Uttar Pradesh. In a number of other States, the District Planning Bodies are headed by officials. Functional decentralisation, in the sense of clearly defining the scope of the planning functions at the district level, has been attempted in these States. There has also been an attempt at the disaggregation of funds at the State level (ranging from 30% in Uttar Pradesh to 45% in Jammu & Kashmir of the total State Plan funds) for allocation amongst the districts. The methodologies for inter district allocation of outlays have also been evolved in these States. Concomitantly, suitable administrative decentralisation measures have also been introduced.

4.6 These are some significant developments. However, 'localism' in planning to the extent that is desired has not come about, since a major portion of the district outlays are apportioned amongst the line departments who make the decisions at the State level about their district-wise allocations. This leaves the district with little or no decision-making powers. Partly to remedy this situation and to confer some decision-making powers to the local level, a few States like Gujarat have made some special provision, by instituting a small quantum of "untied funds", which are meant to be used exclusively for a limited number of small local level planning schemes. In the Gujarat scheme, 20% of the divisible outlay at the State level is set apart for distribution among the districts as 'un-tied fund', of which 15% is meant as discretionary outlay to be utilised by the district planning body for local schemes at its direction. The remaining 5% is intended as an 'incentive grant', payable to the districts, subject to their raising their own resources on a matching basis. The Working Group on District Planning has commended this approach for adoption by other States. The present trends rural that these innovations in district planning are now being sought to be replicated in a number of other Status. This briefly sums up the present stage of the art of District Planning in the country.

4.7 In order to place district planning on a sound and scientific fooling; the planning commission's working group on District Planning had identified certain essential pre-requisites to be fulfilled. These are:

(a) Existence of political will and commitment;
(b) Setting up of District Planning Body in each district;
(c) Setting up a suitable machinery for planning in each district;
(d) Clear demarcation of planning functions;
(e) Disaggregation of plan funds and devolution of financial resources;
(f) Delegation of administrative powers;
(g) Evolution of new patterns of political and administrative behaviour;
(h) Ensuring public participation at all stages in the Planning process; and
(i) Training and re-training of personnel.

4.8 In order that the State in different levels of development may move towards decentralisation over a definite period of time, the District Planning Working Group had advocated a progressive or "stages" approach. The Stage I will be a phase of "initiation", which will involve inter alia, establishing planning procedures, disaggregating outlays between the State and district sectors, evolving criteria for inter-district allocation of plan funds and strengthening of planning capabilities at the district level. Stage-II will be one of "Limited Decentralisation", when planning for certain sectors of activity like MNP, Agriculture and allied activities and all target-group-oriented planning will be brought within the purview of district planning. Granting extensive delegation of powers to the district level will be specially sought to be achieved during this stage. Stage-III will be the final stage, which will encompass planning for all district sector activities. During this stage, a set of wide-ranging administrative, financial and decision-making powers will devolve upon the district and a high level of popular participation will be sought to be achieved. It is envisaged that all States in the country would reach the final phase by the year 2000 A.D. The Working Group had recommended that as far as possible, the States should try to reach this goal even before the time span indicated. This Committee is basically in agreement with the approach to decentralisation indicated by the Working Group on District Planning.

4.9 In order to provide concrete direction to the decentralisation process visualised above, we feel that the establishment of a sound planning and implementation machinery at the district level is crucial. In our view, this planning and implementation machinery must have three major wings. On would be a Planning Cell to carry out the major tasks in district planning, such as preparing a resource inventory, project appraisal and selection, setting of priorities and plan formulation for the district and to perform the review and monitoring functions during the stage of implementation. As suggested by the Planning Commission's Working Group, we also recommend that this planning cell should have a District Planning Officer, assisted by a suitable multi-disciplinary technical team. In our view, the second wing of the District Planning and implementation machinery must be the one concerned with the detailed planning and implementation of all anti-poverty programmes. As has been made clear in this report elsewhere, our concept of a programme of poverty alleviation is something quite different from the one contained in the present IRD Programme. It would embrace the entire gamut of rural development-including all aspects of production, productivity, infrastructure and welfare. Each and every programme concentrating on any aspect of rural development will also have within it, an anti-poverty component or a sub-plan for the poor. Thus it is not merely the productive sectors of the economy like agriculture and small industry, but also other sectors like health, education etc. which would include in them a component exclusively meant for the poor. This wing of the District Planning and implementation machinery will be concerned with the planning and implementation tasks related to all anti-poverty schemes contained in every sector of rural development. We recommended that this wing should consist of a Project Coordinator/Director for anti-poverty programmes with his complement of staff to undertake the micro-level planning tasks envisaged here. The third wing of the District Planning and implementation machinery will be a budgetary and financial control mechanism which will manage the total development activities at the district level from the financial angle. We recommend that a District Finance and Accounts Officer together with his complement of staff should be in control of this Wing. This officer will control both plan and non-plan expenditures in the district. As we have indicated elsewhere in this report, the plan and non-plan distinction should vanish at the district level. There should be considerable delegation of powers (including reappropriation powers) to the District Finance & Account Officer from the State level so that there is smooth channeling of funds to the various developmental activities in the district. We feel that the tripartite planning and implementation machinery set up envisaged here is the most crucial to the success of decentralised planning process at the district level.

4.10 The leads us to the question as to who should be the head of this tripartite development machinery and what should be his status and functions in relation to the existing administrative set up at the district level. The previous committees/Working Groups which have gone into this question have, by and large, recommended the strengthening of the position of the collector in some manner. For instance, the Planning Commission's Working Group on District Planning had emphasised the need for bringing about effective horizontal coordination at the district level by taking action along four major directions. These include: *(a)* strengthening of the position of the Collector; *(b)* Placing the departmental functionaries under the direct administrative control of the Collector by deeming their services as on deputation from their departments; *(c)* making the district officials accountable to the District Planning Body; and *(d)* streamlining and simplifying procedures for according administrative and technical sanctions. In our view, the strengthening of the position of the Collector, either by delegation of more powers to him or by posting of a senior person in the service will not make much of a difference, as long as he is loaded with all developmental functions alongwith his other duties of law and order and revenue. At present, the Collector is heavily over-loaded with multifarious functions. Though most of the developmental activities at the district level are implemented by the various functional/line departments, the Collector as the Chief Executive in the distrit has a central role as the coordinator of all the programmes implemented in the district. This Committee feels that developmental functions at the district level should be separated and entrusted to an officer called the District Development Commissioner who should be much senior in rank to the present District Collector. This, in our opinion, will enable the officer to give undivided attention to development matters and also help establish the primacy of development administration over house keeping functions. Detailed recommendations in this regard are given in Chapter IX of this report.

4.11 It is our view that alongwith the establishment of the office of District Development Commissioner, a significant restructuring of planning and implementation machinery at the district level should also take place. The proliferation of developmental programmes with their own vertical structures and the excessive departmentalization at the district level have been found to be counterproductive to integrated and coordinated development. The District Rural Development Agency specifically established for the implementation of anti-poverty programmes should be gradually phased out and merged into the office of the District Development Commissioner. The services of the principal technical officers at the district level of the various specialized departments should be available to the District Development body headed by the Commissioner. Alongwith the strengthening of District Development Administration, the planning functions at the district level should also be enlarged. There should be a clear demarcation between the planning functions at the state level and the district level. The Planning Commission's Working Group had emphasised this aspect and has called it "functional decentralisation". The district plan should not be simply the district segment of the state plan involving a simple mechanical disaggregation of the state plan schemes. It should be the product of a well conceived and well debated exercise taking full note of the local aspirations and local needs of the district community. In this context, the recommendation made by the Working Group on District Planning for setting up district planning bodies in which adequate representation is provided for the under-privileged ecnomic/occupational/ social groups, voluntary agencies etc. is a very relevant one. We endorse this recommendation.

4.12 The Working Group on District Planning has also recommended that the institutional framework for district planning should be conceived as a social instrument of decision making, which should be a happy blend of local autonomy, administrative capability and planning expertise. In this context, the integration of the Panchayati Raj institutional set up with the district development administration set up is an aspect which cannot be ignored. Our recommendations in this regard have been spelt out in another Chapter (Chapter VI). The Working Group on District Planning had also recommended that "ultimately the Zila Parishads should assume all the planning functions at the district level. Till they develop the capabilities of planning, other arrangements may prevail".

4.13 The question of linking up district planning to the planning at other area levels in the hierarchy of multilevel planning and integrating the district plan into the State plan are issues which are very relevant to decentralised planning and implementation. The level next to the district is the State, although in some bigger States in the country there is also an additional tier called 'Division'. But this level does not perform any planning functions and only acts as a coordinating level. At the time of the formulation of the Seventh Five Year Plan, a vigorous debate was initiated by the Economic Advisory Council to the Prime Minister on the question of introducing an additional tier at the intermediate level between the district and the State to bring about more effective coordination of planning and development activities in the State. We, however, understand that barring some large states in the country (where a divisional set-up already exists). The reaction of most of the States was not quite favourable to this idea. We therefore do not make any recommendations on this question, but would leave it to the decision of the States in accordance with the existing administrative structure in their areas.

4.14 Once the district plans, as envisages here have been prepared, some suitable administrative arrangements should be made to consider them and integrate them into the State Plan. For this purpose, we recommend the setting up of a State Development Council (on the analogy of the National Development council), so that the plans are brought into a common framework. Elsewhere, we have elaborated and discussed this idea. This will establish a healthy dialogue of the districts with the State.

4.15 The decentralised planning concept, when extended to the level below the district would embrace planning at the block or sub-block (i.e., a cluster of villages) and the village levels.

4.16 The major operational machinery for implementation of District Rural Development Plan should be the block level set up. During the years that followed the phasing of the community development programme in the rural areas, the block-level set up has lost its original pre-eminent position in development administration. As in the case of district, at the block level also (though to a lesser extent), there has been proliferation of agencies and programmes over the last three decades. Alongwith this, the complexities and technical content of the various programmes/projects/schemes also have increased. The BDO's office which was expected to serve as a catalyst in the developmental process in the initial years is not in a position to effectively meet the demands on it now. Further, as against an annual budget of a few lakh rupees in the initial years of planning, at present annual investment of over a crore of rupees is being made in a block. This Committee recommends that the Block Development Office should be the sheet-anchor of the entire rural development process but upgraded. The level of the Chief Executive Officer at the Block/Tehsil should be upgraded and designated as an Assistant Development Commissioner. He should be an officer of the status of Sub-Divisional Officer. The detailed recommendations are given in Chapter IXof the report.

4.17 The changes that have occurred in the orientation of planning in recent years have led to an increasing emphasis on micro-level planning involving "community action" and "group action" for the planning of a cluster of families and villages designed for the alleviation of rural poverty and for the provision of services and facilities within easy access of rural settlements. One of the views expressed in this context is that even the present block area is too large a unit for purpose of such planning. A cluster of 10-12 villages with a rural service centre as its focal point is preferred in this context. The Ashoka Mehta Committee has recommended the "Mandal" with a population of about 15,000 people as the suitable unit area below the district for such planning purposes. Some state governments like Andhra Pradesh and Karnataka are trying to introduce this arrangement. It is for the State Governments to decide on the appropriate unit area for planning below the district, taking the various aspects of their current administrative setup into account, including administrative costs and availability of personnel.

4.18 Whatever be the unit area for planning just below the district-block or sub-block-the village continues to be discrete entity for planning from the bottom. It is therefore necessary to consider methods of improving local level participation in planning for rural development at the village level, which is most crucial in this regard. The Village Panchayats must be invigorated for this purpose in the first instance. The Planning Commission has recently documented a success story in rural development in Tamil Nadu in a village called Kundra Kudi.* This study provides considerable insights

*Planning Commission, Towards Improved Local Level Planning for Rural Development, case study of Kuntrakudi, Tamil Nadu, July 1985.

into the factors that have contributed to success in rural development. Stated in terms of broad principles at the level of generality, these are:

(a) Building up a responsible and responsive Receiving Mechanism called 'Village Planning Forum (VPF)', which is a people's institution for planning and development, to provide a forum for various classes of people and interests in the village to interact among themselves and to prepare an acceptable framework for planning.

(b) Ensuring a willing, understanding and adaptive Delivery Mechanism which, in effect, implies bringing about attitudinal changes among the government functionaries engaged in development administration.

(c) Bringing into existence a 'think-tank' or 'Third Party Planner' which can play both an advisory role in planning on a continuous basis, as well as catalyst/ motivational role in implementation with some degree of involvement (not mere association) in the planning and implementation process.

(d) Identifying a local leader of high personal integrity who is respected by all sections of the people and who can integrate the functions mentioned in (a), (b) and (c).

(e) Ensuring a style of functioning (of the planning mechanism) which will be informed by an informal group dynamic approach to decision making and which would be neither compelling nor absorbing in its performance and which would be able to eliminate any conflicts/fluctuations arising during the planning process.

(f) Adoption of flexible procedures and consensus building techniques as well as healthy conventions in the working process.

(g) Devising of a network of informal consultative groups outside the regular institutional mechanism for group action which would expand the scope of public participation and also ensure voluntary agency participation.

(h) Training-both formal and informal for the local youth inducted into the development projects to impart both the skills as well as moral qualities.

4.19 While it is difficult to meet all the requirements stated above in every village context, the idea of institutionalization of village group dynamics and improvement of the capabilities of the "receiving mechanism" through an organisation like "Village planning Forum" can go a long way towards improving local level planning for rural development and result in a better realization of our investment in rural areas. The Committee recommends that the State Governments may take note of the conclusions reached in this study.

4.20 Decentralised planning calls for an immense amount of data and information specially to meet the new orientations in planning that have emerged in recent years. This would mean making improved arrangements for the collection, storing, processing and retrieval of data in a quick manner. Information technologies have vastly improved in recent times. The introduction of the micro processors and the development of relatively cheap standard software for these seem to hold great potential for district planners. State Governments may take note of these developments and consider the introduction of technologies appropriate to their contexts.

4.21 To sum up, decentralised planning at the district level has to be pursued carefully taking into account the various points raised in this Chapter. At the risk of repetition, we may reiterate the following recommendations:

(a) Rural Development represents the major component of District Planning. The concept of rural development that we have adopted in this report is a very comprehensive one and extends beyond the limited scope of the Centrally Sponsored Integrated Rural Development Programme, that is currently being implemented in all the States. It would include all those programmes meant to increase production and raise productivity in the rural areas as well as programmes meant to improve the physical well-being and quality of life of the rural people, such as improved food supplies and nutrition together with basic services such as health and education and basic infrastructure such as expansion of communications and improvement of housing. Since rural development is intended to reduce poverty, every sectoral programme for rural development designed to increase production, raise productivity and to provide basic services must include within it a component exclusively meant for the target groups i.e. the lowest income groups or the rural poor. This would mean that each and every sectoral programme meant for the rural areas will also have something like a sub-plan for the rural poor as part of such programme. Thus the concept of rural development presented here takes a "systems view" of development with a built in strategy for the target groups in the rural areas. In our view, all the various components of rural development should be effectively coordinated under the umbrella of District Planning. By doing so, balanced rural-urban relations may also ensure, as district planning will bring under its purview the planning for small towns also. The Working Group on District Planning had also recommended the inclusion of small towns in district planning.

(b) The District Plan should encompass the total activity in the district. The idea of totality needs some elaboration. It would mean that activities undertaken both under plan and non-plan funds should be taken into account for evaluating performance and projecting needs. Plan after plan, the State Governments have been undertaking development works in each sector like agriculture, animal husbandry, minor irrigation, cooperation, forestry, small and village industries, education, health etc. If this total achievement is not taken into account, truncated planning will ensure and realistic planning will not be possible. The plan, non-plan distinction is meant only for an accounting procedure. For district planning, this distinction should vanish.

(c) We strongly believe that rural development should be responsive to the needs of the rural people. If this should be so, the first and necessary step is to devolve

substantial and effective power to a democratically constituted level of local governance that is concerned with the determination and implementation of rural development programmes. In other words, the Panchayat Raj Institutions should be activised both to provide a forum for the resolution of objective conflicts of interest and a technical organisation for planning and administration that is capable of formulating development plans (in consultation with other government entities) and of carrying them into practice. We further recommend that in order to balance the power of the rich in the PRIs, it must be ensured that their base among the people is rendered sufficiently diverse to allow for the expression and reconciliation of a variety of class and functional interests.

(*d*) In order to give some leeway and maneuverability in planning and decision-making to the District Planning body, it necessary to place some funds at its disposal which are not ties to any departmental schemes and which may be used towards small schemes meant to meet the local priorities, needs and aspirations of the local community. The Gujarat method of providing 'un-tied funds' to the district together with its discretionary and incentive components was referred to earlier. This Committee recommends such an approach for adoption by all State, so as to give the District Planning bodies some role in planning for their local areas. The quantum of such 'un-tied fund' provided to the district should be sizeable, so that it evokes a sense of enthusiasm and responsibility among the local bodies and builds up their capability to plan and manage local-level projects. States could decide the quantum of 'un-tied' funds as their resources would permit.

(*e*) We advocate that there should be a single all embracing planning authority at the district level. This planning authority as we have envisaged above, should be an arm of the Zila Parishad. We recommend that the fragmented planning structures that currently exist at the district level must be gradually used into the planning apparatus envisaged here. This alone would effectively ensure linkages in area development at the district level.

(*f*) We strongly feel that if development administration at the district level is to be rendered effective, the Chief Executive at the district level should be given appropriate authority, control and command over the line officials. The District Collector today who is saddled with law and order, revenue and developmental functions is unable to find adequate time for the latter with the result that coordination at the district level is not effective. We therefore, recommend that there should be a separate senior officer to attend solely to developmental functions. He may be designated as District Development Commissioner. He should be an official much senior to the present District Collector and should possess wide developmental experience. At the Block level, he should be assisted by Assistant Development Commissioners.

(*g*) We feel that the functions of the existing important institutional structures at the district level as well as the linkages and relationships among them need to be rationalised, so that they are non-overlapping and mutually supportive. Such institutional structures identified by us are: (a) the District PRI (wherever it exists), (b) the DRDA, (c) The District Planning Council, and (d) other special development agencies at the district level, e.g. Tribal Development Agency. In Chapter IX we have discussed the organizational structure in which the functions of these institutions/ agencies will be performed by appropriate bodies with a democratic base.

Appendix-III

REPORT OF THE WORKING GROUP ON DISTRICT PLANNING
(VOLUME-1)
CHAPTER 1
CONCLUSIONS & RECOMMENDATIONS

1. To make decentralised planning a success, it has to be backed up by sound practices. The capabilities for decentralised planning have to be assiduously built up, the right procedures and suitable structures have to be evolved and necessary technical and administrative changes, including attitudinal changes have to be brought about among the bureaucrats and the politicians. The various initiatives and improvisations necessary should be introduced cautiously and "in steps", providing adequate time for assimilating them, thus paving the way for learning through experience at every stage and making necessary modifications in the process as we go along. (Para 3.4)

2. For decentralised planning to make headway, institutional mechanisms have to be made more broadbased with the active involvement of local representatives and endowed with a greater degree of autonomy in local decision-making. Simultaneously, several administrative and financial delegations as well as other measures have to be systematically worked out. (Para 3.8)

Concept of District Planning

3. The concept of district planning adopted by the working group is akin to the concept of integrated area planning. (Para 3.11)

4. At the State level, suitable decisions have to be taken about an appropriate inter-dependency mix and proper

function-sharing between the State and District levels taking into account the planning and other capabilities available at the grass roots level. (Para 3.14)

5. The totally of all planning activities at the level of District which is a sub-system would vest with a single District Planning body who would determine the priorities and allocate funds accordingly among the various development sectors. (Para 3.15)

6. The district plan should take into account the regional offinities and should be informed by a regional perspective. It will also be necessary to recognise the sub-regions within the district. (Paras 3.19(1) & 3.19(2))

7. The Panchayati Raj Institutions and other local government institutions should, play crucial role in the district planning process. Ultimately district planning will have to be taken over by these bodies. Therefore, it would be necessary to strengthen them right from now onwards, so that they could play their legitimate role in the district planning process in course of time. [Paras 3.19(3), 5.22, 5.23, 5.32]

8. Though, each district plan must be specific to its own agro-climatic and socio-economic conditions, it must reflect the following basic objectives of the national plan.

(a) Increasing production;

(b) Reducing unemployment; and

(c) Alleviating poverty, (Paras 3.20 & 3.24)

9. With the devolution of more planning functions to the district level the technical planning machinery (both the quality and quantity) will need to be augmented. (Paras 3.20 & 3.24)

9A. It is recommended that the Planning Commission should have a fresh look at the question of staffing the the District Planning Cell in the light of this report and suggest a more realistic staffing pattern avoiding duplication of staff between planning cell and line departments. (Para 4.27)

10. In order to improve upon the system of choosing the right schemes among the numerous suggestions made by several agencies, groups, and individuals, the States could consider the scrutiny of these proposals by a committee of experts before they are placed before District Planning Body. (Para 4.30)

11. Raising the levels of persons lower down the administrative hierarchy is one of the basic necessities and

this could be tackled by inducting some high caliber technical staff into the district planning machinery and frequently organising training and refresher courses for the lower staff on a regular and continuing basis. (Para 4.40)

12.Evaluation should be undertaken by an independent agency, and not by the District Planning body. It could be done at the State's level or by any independent agency. Evaluation should not be confined to a project/scheme but the planning act as such should be evaluated on an annual basis. (Paras 4.16 & 10.11)

Prerequisites for District Planning

13. The essential prerequisites for decentralised district planning will include, apart from political commitment, defining the scope and content of a district plan some measures for the dis-aggregation of allocations, delegations of administrative and financial powers, evolution of new patterns of administrative behaviour, a reorientation of attitudes and relationships, building up of a capabilities and instruments of control, establishment of participatory structures and umbrella mechanisms, and continuous and retraining of personnel. (Para 5.2)

14.The Working Group, strongly recommends that there should be no bar for incurring some essential maintenance expenditure from plan funds to revive and rehabilitate some languishing investments. (Para 5.3)

15. The Working Group commends the adoption of a twofold classification of scheme into district level and state-level schemes by the States. (Para 5.4)

Disaggregation of Outlays

16. In the allocation of funds between the state and the districts, the guiding principle should be that while local priorities must receive importance in the district plan, they should not be at the cost of overriding national and state priorities. Keeping this in view the disaggregation of plan funds from the State to District level may be done by providing for major State Sector schemes and then derive the District Sector outlay as residuary of this. Alternatively provide for all the District Sector programmes in the first instance and treat State Sector as residuary. Perhaps the exercise could be

conducted from both ends to reconcile the figures. However the proportion thus arrived at should not be made the basis for making future allocations, as this would leave little or no scope for the districts to take up new schemes. Therefore, any proportion arrived at by a State should not be continued on a permanent basis, but should be constantly watched in a dynamic context and revised. The revision may be carried out say every five years. (Paras 4.12 & 5.8)

17. The Working Group recommends that the divisible plan outlays may be distributed among the districts on the basis of three elements. Viz., population, area and level of development. Each state may work out its own criteria for giving weightage for allocation of outlays on account of level of development. (Para 5.10)

18. Vesting the district planning body with all powers to divide the sectoral allocations in the district is an ideal goal which can be reached only at some distant point of time. In the meantime some special steps must be taken to give some scope to the district planning body to undertake a few local development programmes on its own to meet local aspirations and requirements. This could be done by making a discretionary allocation to the district planning body.

(Para 5.11)

19. In its allocation formula for the transfer of Plan funds for the district level, Gujarat has set aside a small proportion (5%) as incentive grants to match efforts made at the district level for additional mobilisation of local resources in kind and/or money. The Working Group commends this approach for emulation by other States. (Para 5.12)

20. So far as the relatively underdeveloped districts in a State are concerned, their cause would be adequately served by giving proper weightage to the various criteria of backwardness in the allocation formula, rather than by treating them on a separate footing. (Paras 5.14 & 6.40)

21.The reduction of intra-district imbalances should be the aim in the allocation of district resources among the blocks. States should evolve their own methods for this purpose. In districts, where special problems are met within some blocks, some special dispensation may become necessary. (Para 5.15)

Organisational Framework

22. The institutional frame work for District Planning

should be a social instrument of decision making which would be a happy blend of local autonomy, administrative capability and planning expertise. (Para 5.16)

23. In District Planning bodies, the collector must play the role of the Chief Coordinator. To enable him to discharge these responsibilities properly and efficiently he must have the necessary status, powers and responsibilities. He should be able to effect the necessary horizontal and vertical coordination in the planning and implementation tasks. In order to move towards this goal, the departmental functionaries must be considered as on deputation from their respective departments and posted to the District Planning bodies. In this way they will be made responsible for implementation of their respective programmes at the district level and will be held accountable for their performance to the District Planning bodies. This is no doubt a major structure re-organisation. But such changes are very necessary if the District Planning process is to be made effective.(Para 5.21)

24. As regards administrative decentralisation, the Working Group recommends that the procedure for administrative and technical sanctions should be so simplified and streamlined that none of the district level reappropriation within minor heads of account should also be vested with the Collector. Only matters beyond the prescribed limits of sanction or reappropriation should be referred to Finance/Planning Department. In other words, the accent should be on bulk control rather than on detailed control. (Para 5.24)

25. It is important that district level functionaries are brought under the control of the District Collector who should be the sheet anchor of implementation of district plans. To ensure the compliance of district level departmental functionaries, their confidential reports in respect of district sector performance should be written by the District Collector which should form part of the personal files of concerned officers. (Para 5.25)

26.Since the Collector's association with the developmental work is a must, it is suggested that a senior officer of the rank of Additional Collector may be provided in each district to assist the Collector and to relieve him of much of the routine responsibilities. (Para 5.27)

27. The size of the districts should also be made more

manageable purely on administrative grounds. (Para 5.28)

28. The Departmental officers at the district level should not be subjected to frequent transfers. They should normally be kept in one district for a minimum period of three years. (Para 5.28)

29. Officers serving in remote or inaccessible districts could be paid special pay upto 35% of their salaries. Residential accommodation and other minimum facilities should also be made available in such areas. (Para 5.28)

30.Suitable adjustments must be made in the budgetary format and Demands for Grant of the state to display district plan outlay to ensure accountability to the legislature. Within each Demand, a Minor Head called 'District Sector Schemes' may be opened. (Para 5.29)

31. An additional document called the Annual District Plan should be placed before the legislature along with other budget papers. This document should contain district-wise information on annual plan in terms of Minor Heads and subheads. Listing of each individual scheme and the detailed heads may be avoided. (Para 5.29)

32. Within the framework of multi-level planning, the functions of the District Planning Bodies should be (I) crystallization of local needs and objectives, (II) taking stock of the natural and human endowments, (III) listing and mapping of amenities, (IV) formulation of district plans, (V) formulation of policies, programmes and priorities, (VI) coordinated implementation, and (VII) monitoring and review of the implementation of district plans and programmes. (Para 5.30)

33. The District Planning Body should consist of a Chairman, Member-Secretary and a reasonable number of members, say 50. The size and composition of the District Planning Body should be decided by the State Governments. (Para 5.31)

34. In addition to the District Planning Body, it would be desirable to have a smaller Executive Body which will be in the nature of a Steering Committee. (Para 5.33)

35. For the District Planning Bodies statutory sanction is not necessary. These bodies may be constituted under an executive order of the State Government as has been done in most states in the country. (Para 5.33)

36. The District Planning Cell should be headed by a Chief

Planning Officer whose status in the district should be next only to that of the District Collector/District Development Commissioner. On recruitment he should be specially trained in regional/area planning methodology and techniques. (Para 5.35)

37. The Chief Planning Officer should be assisted by an able team of experts drawn from various disciplines like economics, statistics, agronomy, cartography, economic geography, engineering, sociology, banking etc., as well as from subject areas like agriculture, animal husbandry, horticulture and so on. The actual size and composition of this team should be left to the district. (Para 5.36)

38.There should also be a Planning Officer of BDO's rank at the block level assisted by two Research Assistants and a Typist and a messenger to help the Chief Planning Officer to coordinate the Block Level Programmes with regard to intra-Block gaps in development and amenities. (Para 5.37)

39. A competent unit for District Planning should be established at the state level to complement and bolster the planning capacity at the District level. (Para 5.38)

40. There should be one single planning cadre for the state comprising of the technical planning staff at the block, district and state levels. (Para 5.39)

Training

41.Those who man the District Planning Organisations should be given a more intensive and broad based training in relevant areas like Economics, statistics, concepts and techniques of comprehensive, spatial sectoral and project planning. They should also be well-grounded in analytical and evaluative techniques. (Para 5.40)

42.At the Centre, the Department of Personnel (Training Wing) must come forward in a big way not merely to organise the training of trainers in the apex level institutions in the country, but also to assist the state training institution to equip themselves for the training tasks. (Para 5.42)

43. We recommend that the Department of Personnel (Training Wing) in collaboration with the Planning Commission should set up in group to work out the curriculum as well as the modalities for a properly conceived training programme for district planning trainees at different levels. (Para 5.43)

Methodology of District Planning

44. The methodology of district planning should be simple and the district plan itself concrete, specific and practical. (Para 6.2)

45. Following steps in sequence for the formulation of the district plans are suggested. This would in fact be the simple methodology to be adopted for district planning.

(a) Formulation of the major objectives of the district plan.

(b) Compilation of data for district planning.

(c) Bringing out the profile of the district in relation to the basic objectives.

(d) Formulating the main strategy and thrust of district planning.

(e) Analysis of the existing programmes and projects with reference to the strategy outlined.

(f) Assessment of resources for allocation to various programmes and projects.

(g) Statement of physical and financial components of the district plan.

(h) Statement of spatial dimensions of the district plan.

(i) Relationships and links between the district plan and regional and state development plans. (Para 6.6)

46. The suggested methodology of district planning, which is normative, assumes that the district sector, which may not be true for all the states at present. It is, therefore, necessary to make it clear that all the procedures outlined here would be applicable only at a stage when fulfledged district planning would be possible. (Para 6.7)

47. The District Plan must consist of integration of development activities in primary, secondary, tertiary and infrastructure sectors so as to deal with the problem of unemployment and poverty. Full employment is both an objective of planning and also the means of reducing poverty and increasing production. The district plan must essentially provide for expansion and diversification of the economy so as to reduce poverty and increase employment. (Paras 6.10, 6.13 & 6.14)

48. While dealing with the problem of poverty and unemployment, the district plan must focus on providing

gainful employment opportunities to small and marginal farmers, agricultural labourers and artisans. (Para 6.15)

49. The data for district planning should be in relation to the four sectors of the economy and the various sections of the society which have been mentioned above. (Para 6.16)

50.Necessary minimum amount of data and information necessary for planning and decision-making at the district level should be identified and data should be collected. (Para 6.17)

51. It is suggested that the collection of data/information by the district planning team must cover all those areas defined as the 'District Sector' including such background information, as may be helpful in their meaningful interpretation. An illustrative list of data/information useful for district planning is shown in Annexure 6.1. (Para 6.18)

52. States are advised to adjust their data requirements depending on the scope to be given by them for district planning and taking into account the analytical abilities of their planning teams. (Para 6.19)

53. The Group feels that regarding income and consumption levels of population and employment and unemployment, to start with, the district planning exercise may incorporate the results of NSS and IRDP Surveys as area readily available duly cross-checked with other information and refined to the extent possible; but gradually the NSS data should be made usable by introducing the required changes in the sampling pattern. (Para 6.21)

54. On technology and productivity, the information has to be obtained from various sources, including from some spot surveys, if necessary. In order to obtain data relating to inflows and outflows of goods and services, it would be necessary to build up regional accounts at the district level on a systematic and continuous basis. The Central Statistical Organisation should initiate this process with the active assistance of States. The Group notes that the C.S.O. had set up a Committee on Regional Accounts in 1972 and the report was given in 1976. The recommendations of this Committee should be quickly implemented. (Para 6.22)

55. The Working Group recommends that Districtwise estimation of income originating' should be attempted by all States. In the mean time, whatever information is available and used in the planning exercise. (Para 6.23)

56. The data base could be greatly strengthened by the utilisation of technological tools like aerial photo interpretation and remote-sensing technology. We suggest that for every district in the country, the thematic maps may be prepared. (Para 6.24)

57. As aerial photographs will be required for an exceedingly important national task, the Defence Ministry should relax their regulations and make them available without delays. The planning Commissions should identify suitable educational and other research institutions in the country where such work could be carried out and should provide adequate funds to these institutions to undertake this work. (Para 6.25)

58.The data collected would then provide what we call the profile of the district and would itself suggest the strategy for development which is particularly relevant to that district. The district planners must have a total and comprehensive perspective of the district and a district profile would only emerge from such a comprehensive perception of the planners of the needs and potentialities of the district.

(Para 6.26 & 6.27)

59. When District planning becomes a full-fledged and independent operation at the district level, working out the area strategies for the district and its sub-regions will constitute the most important step and the content of the plan must be derived from these strategies. (Para 6.28)

60. The existing or ongoing schemes must be subjected to very close scrutiny in terms of suitability of these schemes to the specific conditions of the district; and if on scrutiny they need to be modified to suit the requirements of the district they should be suitably modified. The central or centrally sponsored schemes or even State schemes should provide for sufficient flexibility to take note of the varying local requirement and the district planners must have the freedom to suggest local modifications in the schemes on the basis of close scrutiny of how the schemes have actually worked. Also a district plan must provide for replacement of the existing scheme with new schemes or supplementing existing schemes with new schemes. (Para 6.29)

61.Intelinkages between various programmes and projects are extremely important though these are overlooked, with the result that individual plan schemes do not fructify in the absence of backup from supporting programmes. Indeed, successful implementation of programme require that all the forward and backward linkages are properly taken care of. (Para 6.30)

62. One of the persisting weaknesses of planning in India is the implementation gap between what is aimed at and what is accomplished. It is the specific responsibility of district planning to fill up the implementation gap. District plan should take note of various leakages that prevent the impact of plan programmes being felt. The plan programmes must contain proposals for strengthening organisation and management which should prevent such a leakage. (Para 6.31)

63. At present the block may be considered as the unit area for eliminating intra-district disparities. To arrive at intra-district variations suitable indicators may be developed. (Para 6.32)

64. The District Planners' task would be rather focused on setting priorities among the numerous project schemes ideas thrown up during his resource inventory and other analyses and those that emerged during his discussions with the public as to felt needs. His choice among different candidate projects has to rest on other considerations that the quantified efficiency evaluation. (Para 6.36)

65. The district planning should be an attempt to dovetail the various resources for different projects and schemes in an integrated manner. (Para 6.39)

66. While drawing up a programme for the development of specific activities, it would be desirable to look at them not as unrelated or individual items by themselves but in terms of their inter-relationship with other related, subsidiary or supplmenetary activities and to draw up plans for all the related activities in an integrated manner. (Paras 6.50 & 6.51)

67. The final plan should contain the tentative cost of each project and programme, summary of the mode of implementation, actions needed by the various agencies, the system of financial control and monitoring methods during the course of implementation and final evaluation. In the District plan, all projects and schemes should be fully reflected, with all their inter-relationship, interdependencies and complementaries duly worked out. (Para 6.55)

68. It must be ensured that the district plan fits in the frame work the State Plan and the National Plan. The sectoral allocations as emerging from the various district plans in the States must add with the budgetary allocations made sectorise at the State level. (Para 6.56)

69.The draft plan drawn up as above should be placed before the District Planning Body (Board or Council, whatever be its nomenclature) and fully discussed and finalised. The district plan emerging in this manner should then be forwarded to the State Government for being dovetailed into the State Plan. (Para 6.57)

70.There should be a time-table for planning in the state. The District Planning Officer should be given adequate time, say about 3 months to formulate the District Plan with some degree of thoroughness. The District Planning Bodies should finalise their annual plans for the ensuing year during the second half of October. (Para 6.58)

71. In the light of objectives set out for district planning, it could be realistic to think in terms of three kinds of District Plans in relation to different time spans. These would be:

(a) Perspective Plan-covering 10 to 15 years;

(b) Five Year Plans;

(c) Annual Plans (Para 6.59)

72. A simultaneous movement in all these directions though desirable may not be feasible. The minimum expertise made available for District Planning may be initially directed towards the formulation of a medium term plan coinciding with the Seventh Five Year Plan alongwith its annual breakup. In States, where the pre-requisites for District Planning are already established, the annual plan exercise for the district may commence even from 1984-85 onwards. Other States, where the District Planning infrastructure and the essential pre-requisites have not been established, should start providing for these from 1984-85 onwards so that District Planning could be initiated positively from the beginning of the Seventh Plan in all the States in the country. (Para 6.60)

73.It is recommended that the experiments made in the State of Maharashtra, Tamil Nadu, Jammu & Kashmir, Karnataka and Andhra Pradesh in respect of Perspective planning may be carefully studied by the State desiring to embark up district perspective plans so that various pitfalls characterizing these exercises could be avoided. (Para 6.67)

74.The immediate objective should be to attempt district five year plans co-terminus with the 7th Five Year Plan. These district plans should be formulated in all the district of the country. It would be a time bound task entrusted to the district administration. The work for the preparation of district plans, we recommend, should be immediately taken on hand because at least a period of one year would be required for the formulation of the five year district plans. (Para 6.68)

Manpower Planning

75. Man power Planning and budgeting should be for the district as a whole with reference to all the activities (plan, non-plan, developmental and non-developmental) and cannot be confined only to activities included in the District Plan and implemented thereunder. (Paras 6.42, 7.4 and 7.41)

76. In dealing with manpower and employment problems at the district level it was recognised that those categories of manpower who were specialized and highly technical like Doctors, Engineers and Architects would be outside the purview of the district planning process except for their development and utilisation within the district.

(Paras 6.41 and 7.5)

77. The large mass of unskilled manpower would be the main pre-occupation of the planning process at the district level in terms of providing employment and raising their levels of living. It is also recognised that except under special circumstances that except under special circumstances this mass of work force is not mobile and employment opportunities have, therefore, to be found for them in or near the villages where they reside. (Para 6.43 and 7.5)

78. In-between highly skilled and unskilled categories lies the intermediate group for occupations requiring a minimum level of education and some training. Although it is not necessary, nor perhaps desirable, to attempt to provide employment to all such persons within the district there must be skills and occupations which can be wholly confined to the district both in terms of source as well as employment. Every district should be able to identify such categories and make attempts at being self-contained in respect of these by and large. (Paras 6.41 and 7.6)

79. To encourage employers to provide inplant training not only to their employees but also to others, the feasibility of granting concessions or assistance could be examined.

(Para 7.7)

80. A scheme for the improvement of language among matriculates may perhaps be useful alongwith abolition of degree qualification for such jobs where matriculation or Higher Secondary certificate would otherwise, be adequate.

(Para 7.7)

81. Successful experiments have been earned out in giving special training to drop-outs at VIIIth Standard stage and enabling them to be absorbed as salaried worker or to set them up as self-employed workers. Some innovative schemes should be included in the District Plan for this purpose. (Para 7.8)

82. Where employment of children in occupations prohibited by law continues or where employment of children is considered otherwise hazardous or dangerous, the attempt must be to stop such employment of child labour and at the same time provide alternative employment opportunities, wherever necessary, for such displaced children.(Para 7.10)

83. While child labour in general should be gradually phased out, this should be done particularly carefully where they are employed to augment the family income and also where they gain skills in traditional occupations. (Para 7.10)

84. The district level planning process will have to take note of the need for finding employment opportunities for the physically handicapped. (Para 7.11)

85. It is necessary to identify low wage and or high unemployment (Chronic unemployment) areas within the district and take appropriate investment decisions to enable such areas to come up, both in rates of wages and levels of employment. As departmental budgets may not be adequate to meet the requirements of such pockets, the need for a Free Fund from out of which suitable programmes could be financed for such areas becomes strong. Another way of directing attention to these areas will be to confine expenditure under NREP to such areas; alternatively increased allocation of funds could be made under NREP to these areas (Para 6.44 & 7.12)

86. The Working Group recommends that Man power and Employment Planning exercises should be taken up by all States in the country with whatever data and capabilities that exist. (Para 7.15 & 7.17)

87. The Working Group recommends that the district level Census figures may be made available without further delay. Apart from this it would be useful if the census with special reference to employment and make this data available without delay up to district level. (Para 7.19)

88. It would be desirable to make effort to increase the size of the sample so that the NSSO is able to generate reliable district level estimates. (Para 7.20)

89. It is also necessary to devise measures so that results of sample surveys are available at the district level with minimum delay and, in any event, within 12 to 18 months of the completion of these surveys. (Para 7.22)

90. It is desirable that NSSO takes up employment surveys annually, on a regional basis; the State should then be requested to work out, making use of the State Samples, employment situation in different spheres. (Para 7.22)

91. Manpower planning at the district level is essentially directed to those intermediate categories of workers whose functions lie between the level of an unskilled worker on the one hand and an engineer or a technologist or a doctor on the other. (Para 7.26)

92. The extent of unemployment ay be estimated by one of the following methods:

(a) NSSO method suitably modified:
(b) Family labour budget survey of sample households;
(c) Registration method.

The demand, so identified, has to be projected for the next five years. Based on the availability of resources in the District/Block and the potential for nes activities, suitable locations (growth centres) into which these jobs may go may be determined. (Paras 7.27-7.29)

93. All schemes operating in the block or district and directly managed by public sector authorities should be listed, categories and summed up as on a specific date, so that the bench mark information could be updated. (Para 7.34)

94. At the village level, it is necessary to build up in formation on items like housing population, net area sown, the proportion of net area sown to net area irrigated, number of bore wells, number of handlooms, powerlooms, mat weaving units, artisans, the distance to various locations like railway station, bus stop, post office etc. (Para 7.34)

95. District Manpower and Employment Generation Councils (DMPEGC) should function as an important arm of the District planning agency and should be responsible to the latter for formulation of proposals for all employment generation activities in a district. It is necessary that the DMPEGCs are constituted as part of the District Planning Authority. (Para 7.36)

96. To make DMPEGC functionally effective, it should be adequately staffed with experts in different fields. The

membership of the Council should also be broad-based and reflect the pressing need for increasing employment opportunities particularly among the relatively more disadvantaged i.e. Scheduled Castes, Scheduled Tribe, Women, Physically handicapped etc. (Para 7.36)

97. For working out the manpower and employment policies for the district a cadre of manpower experts is required to be built up either by fresh recruitment and training or by giving intensive training to existing District Employment Officers, at selected institutions. (Para 7.38)

98. The exercise on the district manpower and employment plan should get initiated atleast two years before the commencement of the plan period. (Para 7.39)

99. It is also necessary to give some training or at least orientation, to the various departmental functionaries, so that they are able to understand the context in which and the purpose for which information is sought for from them. (Para 7.41)

100. In an environment of increasing economic activity, it is likely that consequent on the vertical mobility in occupations by way of promotions, there is likely to result a deterioration in the level of the skills all along the line. This becomes accentuated, when there is any sudden expansion of employment opportunities in projects. In such a case, it would be necessary to introduce a suitable system of upgradation of skills to maintain standards at all levels. (Para 7.44)

101. In respect of the large number of unskilled manpower, it necessary that the District Manpower Planning and Employment Generation Council in collaboration with other agencies should work out arrangements by which, even in respect of these persons, their capabilities are increased resulting to higher productivity on the kind of jobs that they do. The tendency to import more efficient manpower from outside can also be checked if in implementation of such programs at the local level the practice of entrusting the work to contractors is progressively replaced and organisations like labour cooperatives encouraged to take up these works; alternatively, the works could be executed departmentally. With reference to Scheduled Castes and Scheduled Tribes, specific steps are to be develop entrepreneurial skills among the educated unemployed, so that the employment-oriented schemes are realistically covered and implemented for the

benefit of these sections of our population. (Para 7.45)

102. It is necessary to have a look at the various legislative provisions as well as regulations that may unwittingly come as disincentives to taking up activities which are particularly employment intensive Contrawise specific legislative support may be needed in cases where attempts to create additional employment opportunities are thwarted by recalcitrant minority to take up such programmes. (Para 7.46)

103. The anxiety for increasing, employment opportunities must take account of considerations of ecology and the need, for the protection and improvement of the environment. (Para 7.47)

104. Existence of established practices of interdistrict and intradistrict migration of working population should be taken note of in drawing up manpower and employment plans. (Para 7.48)

105. The District Planning authorities should have sizeable funds which they can, in their discretion, utilise subject to broad guidelines that the State Government may issue to these authorities. The guidelines for the use of free fund should give priority for its use in providing missing links and for fulfillment of the programme of minimum needs and such items in the New 20 Point Programme as are relevant at district level. Further, it may be stipulated that free fund should be used on public works and not for liberalising existing patterns of assistance of the schemes. However, where the basic minimum needs are largely met, the funds may be used for increasing the number of beneficiaries under any existing or future, scheme, but conforming to the prescribed pattern of assistance. (Para 7.49 & 7.50)

106. The endeavour must be to provide full employment to the total working population of the district till the end of the century. Even if this should not become possible, the endeavour should certainly be to increase employment opportunities at a specified percentage during each plan period. (Para 7.51)

107. Within the programmes in the next ten or fifteen years, special attention will have to be given to increasing employment opportunities for women at a rate, which is much higher than the average for the district. Likewise during this period every effort should be taken to ensure a complete elimination of child labour in all these occupations which are prohibited by law, or which are considered hazardous for

dangerous. (Para 7.51)

108.A long term programme of operations relating to say expansion of irrigation, desilting of irrigation tanks, deepening of wells, maintenance of soil conservation works, maintenance and upgrading of roads and like, which are labour—intensive should be drawn up and suitably incorporated in the Five Year Plans and the Annual Plans. (Para 7.52)

109. Projections of changes in population, as well as in the work force, including their sex distribution, will have to be worked out and a long term plan which would take note of the increasing demands for employment drawn up. (Para 7.53)

110. A programme for entrepreneurial development, more-particularly in the small towns in the rural areas, both among the women and the youth will have to be formulated. An important aspect of self-employment programmes can be the need for providing self-employment opportunities for part of the day particularly for women. An important elements of any attempt to improve self-employment activities will be the provision of an adequate and efficient marketing arrangement for the finished/semi-finished products. (Para 7.54)

111. The requirements, both in numbers as well as in categories of skilled and other manpower for any central or state level project that may be implemented in the district, will have to be ascertained and advance action taken, wherever, necessary, to make such skilled manpower available. (Para 7.55)

112. The long-term strategy should, in short, be not merely one of using the available manpower for implementing existing schemes and programmes but to devise such schemes and programmes as would usefully employ the manpower that is available and that would be developed. (Para 7.57)

Spatial Planning

113. A major task to be accomplished through the exercise of spatial planning would be to design a pattern of settlements for human activities. (Para 7.67)

114. Wherever the physical, social and economic characteristics of a district so requires, there should be no hesitation to sub-divide it on the basis of different criteria keeping in view particularly planning objectives. (Para 7.69)

115. Given the size-distribution of settlements in a district and the population and distance threshold for different functions, there will be three main categories of settlements; those which have, those which have, those which do not have should have the function, and those which do not and need not have it. While it is the task of the planner to ensure that all settlements of the second category have the functions warranted by the accepted norms for their location, it is an equally important task for him to ensure that the last category of settlements has access to such functions. In the first category of settlements there could also be some which have the function though they may not be entitled to have them. In their case the planner will not ordinarily disturb the status quo unless he considers relocation desirable and feasible. (Para 7.89)

116.A distinction should be made between functions which are provided by the State and those provided by the private sector. (Para 7.90)

117. In ensuring that functional dependence is established between three categories of settlements described in para 7.89, the planner should take into consideration convenience of access in terms of time and cost burdens passed on to the users. (Para 7.92)

118. The planner should identify gaps between prevailing and required levels of availability of different functions in the district (Functional gap). (Para 7.94)

119.The planner should also identify settlements where new or additional functions are required to be located to reduce the functional gaps. (Para 7.95)

120.Apart from existing functional gaps the planner should also anticipate emerging functional gaps. (Para 7.96)

121. If together the combined population of all settlements in the area can sustain a particular function, the real gap can be eliminated by providing the function at an appropriate location within the area. (Para 7.97)

122. Information relating to the explicit space preference shown by inhabitants of individual settlements in the study area with regard to their movements to avail different functions may have to be generated though field surveys for the purpose of special planning. (Para 7.102)

123. The use of maps in spatial planning is indispensable. The basic requirements is the latest available topographical map(s) of the Survey of India of the scale 1:50,000-1:2,50,000.

The final choice of the scale of the map will depend on the area to be covered and the convenience of use. Another essential map is the revenue map of the Taluk/Sub-division showing village boundaries. (Para 7.103)

124. It is necessary that before the spatial planning exercise commences, the special planner acquaints himself with the objectives of the district Plan, its priorities—the norms prescribed for different functions and the resource constraints. He should also be acquainted with the general socio-economic conditions the district and with its relationship with other districts in the State. [Para 7.107 (i)]

125. Another important preliminary step is the determinations of spatial units of planning which the planner will consider that is cluster of villages, Panchayats, parts of blocks, etc. Likewise, wherever possible spatial planning objective should be quantified and the time frame for planning be defined. [Para 7.107 (ii)]

126. It is desirable to collect and store data in formats which will help in quick retrieval and updating. (Para 7.108)

127. While the data are being collected and processed base maps of the study area can be prepared. (Para 7.109)

128. After the data have been collected and processed and the base maps are ready, the spatial plan should undertake various analysis including those of planning of hierarchy of centres and service areas. (Para 7.109-111)

129. The District Plan should incorporate projections, of population, of production levels and of demand for different functions in its proposals. Applying appropriate techniques, future scenarios and terminal states of important sectors should be projected and their spatial planning implications in corporated in the proposed plan. [Para 7.112(i)]

130. The requirement of functions in the study area should be expressed both quantitatively and qualitatively, taking into account functions which should exist but are absent, those which are not adequately available, as also units of functions which are due for replacement because of depreciation and obsolescence. These quantitative and qualitative estimates should be expressed in specific spatial terms, that is, for individual villages, clusters of villages, service centres of different levels, etc. [Para 7.112(ii)]

131. The proposals of the spatial plan regarding expansion of functions in the study area should take into account the requirements of small towns such as those having Nagar

Panchayats and Notified Area Committees. [Para 7.112(iii)]

132. Where the spatial planner is aware that potentially good alternative proposals exist, it is desirable to indicate the range of choices rather than arbitrarily select only one of them. [Para 7.112(iv)]

133. The spatial planner should recommended inter-se priorities and phasing of implementation of his proposals. [Para 7.112(v)]

134. Detailed costing of alternative proposals should be done in consultation with the concerned subject matter specialists on the district planning team. [Para 7.112(vi)]

135. Assessment of the impact of the proposals on the local ecology/environment should be made for those proposals which entail major changes such as in the physiographic hydrological geological characteristics. [Para 7.112(vii)]

136. To the extent possible, the spatial planning proposals at the district, block, Panchayat and village levels should be kept within existing administrative boundaries to minimise jurisdictional overlap and friction in their implementation. [Para 7.112(viii)]

137. It is possible to adopt spatial planning in two graduated phases. The first stage may consist of preparation of some maps depicting present level of development blockwise and cartographic depiction of the infrastructure taking village as the unit as well as interblock comparison of the level of facilities of selected items. In the second stage, more sophisticated exercises involving determination of hierarchy of centres and service areas and working out of thresholds and norms etc. can be undertaken. (Para 7.114-7.117)

Integrated Planning and Coordinated Implementation

138. Integration has to be worked out carefully and consciously at the stage of plan formulation itself, i.e. at the level at which schemes are formulated, whether at district, block, village or household levels. For integration at the planning stage to come about in the ideal manner the entire planning activity touching on all aspects should be undertaken by one single planning body which will prepare comprehensive plans for all activities at the district level in an objective manner. But this is a long term goal. As we cannot erase the numerous existing structures which are now

performing the planning functions for their limited areas, we have to advance towards final goal in some definite stages and sequences. We have to take note of the existing administrative set-up and the different agencies involved in various development tasks and to work out the appropriate modalities for bringing about integration during the planning stage itself. (Paras 8.7 & 8.8)

139. The role of the Collector in the task of coordination at the District level is very important. (Paras 5.2 & 8.9)

140. The District Planning Body would essentially function as an umbrella organisation nesting the plans of individual departments and agencies and integrating them into a common and consistent framework, sub-serving a central strategy formulated for the district as a whole. (Para 8.11)

141. It is particularly emphasised that the Central Ministries should not encourage the emergence of new agencies and all planning functions should, in future, be the responsibility of the District Planning Body. The Working Group would, therefore, like to emphasis that during the 7th Plan, efforts should be directed towards increasingly devolving the planning functions now being performed by different organisations and agencies to the DPBs so that they will ultimately emerge as the Apex Planning Bodies at the District level. (Para 8.14)

142. The Working Group, recommends that the powers to allocate funds among the various sectoral departments and to make reappropriation within certain limits should be accorded to the District Planning bodies. (Para 8.16)

143. Various poverty alleviation programmes if they are to confer anticipated benefit on a sustained basis have to be provided with considerable external support. The concerned departments must be fixed with the responsibilities for providing such support by incorporating the same in their annual plans. Since it is important to provide the necessary inputs at the proper time, the entire exercise of planning for input and infrastructural support must be completed before April/May. (Para 8.17)

144. The support needed for the poverty alleviation schemes should be worked out in advance for the entire

seventh plan period by adopting an incremental approach. (Para 8.19)

145. The DRDAs should not be only do their internal coordination, but also learn to dialogue effectively with the District Planning Bodies, so that the present vacuum in coordination is effectively bridged. The development dialogue between DRDA and DPB could be institutionalised by providing for mutual representation in these bodies. (Para 8.20)

146. Projects and schemes being implemented in the district have to be coordinated both from the sectoral and locational points of view. Besides, it is also important to harmonise the projects and schemes in time, i.e. to set a coordinated time-schedule for their execution. (Para 8.21)

147. Integration between the District Plan and plans originating from the lower and higher levels has to be brought about though the introduction of effective development dialogue among the planning bodies at various levels. (Para 8.22)

148. Block level planning is necessary to ensure the development of pockets of backwardness and to bring about a more balanced development within the district. In order to ensure integration of block plans with the district plan, the block planning should also be entrusted to District Planning Team. Besides, the district plan should also take note of the special programmes like the tribal sub-plan, for the provision of several complementarities i.e. the input and the infrastructural facilities which are required as a back-up support to these plans. (Para 8.23)

149. For dovetailing the district plans with the State plan the Working Group recommends the following alternatives for the States to consider:—

(a) The Districts need not wait for indication about resource ceiling and can go ahead with planning on an ad-hoc assumption of a 10% step up. They may also draw up a second short list of schemes that could be considered if more resources become available.

(b) The State may take a decision that the District Plan component of the State Plan would be kept in tact whatever be the outcome about outlays after the discussions with the Planning Commission.

(c) The district plan may be a composite plan for medium term, i.e., 5 years with clear annual break-up for the five years sectorwise which should be provided for in the State Plan with very little variations. There can be a second look at the provision of funds at District level as a mid-term review to correct any imbalances. (Para 8.24)

150. In order that the District Credit Plans are realistic, the States should disaggregate the district-wise outlays and present them in State Annual Plans so that the information of the District Credit Plans would become available in November of the previous year. (Para 8.26)

151. The District Credit Plan should also cover the activities of the private sector and give analysis of bankwise position of resource deployment. Reconstitution of the District Coordination Committees and Standing Committee into Compact forums should be expedited. Besides it is necessary to ensure up-to-date land records easy availability of non-encumbrance certificates etc. (Para 8.27)

Rural Urban Integration

152. The Working Group recommends that towns with a population of less than 10,000 should be treated as an integral part of the district area for purposes of overall planning and implementation of development programmes in the district. With such integration, it is also necessary to ensure that the funds provided at the state level for urban development sector are duly disaggregated on a proportional basis for meeting the cost of the urban services of urban centres thus brought into the rural framework of district plan. (Paras 8.28 & 8.29)

153. Benefits under programmes like IRD available to the rural poor should be extended to urban poor living in towns up to a population of 10,000. (Para 8.30)

154. It is necessary to tie up the potential of emerging industrial townships, mining complexes, large irrigation projects and hydel and thermal projects in the midst of rural areas with the development of rural hunterland. (Para 8.31)

155. Representation should be given to the urban local bodies in the District Planning Boards entrusted with the task of formulation of District Plan. [Para 8.34(1)]

156. Urban Local Bodies having a population of over 10,000 should be asked to prepare Annual and Five Year Plans within the Framework of the State Plan. [Para 8.34(3)]

157. In the case of Urban area which will serve as growth centres the linkages between the needs of these areas and plans for meeting these needs by conscious efforts taken up in the adjoining rural areas should be clearly spelt out. [Para 8.38(4)]

People's Participation

158. Some experiments in local level planning through the local people have been made in different State. The Comprehensive Area Development programme tried in West Bengal, Tilonia experiment in Rajasthan. Maliwada experiment in Maharashtra, the Mafatlal Group experiment (Uruli Kanchan etc.) in Maharashtra are some of the examples. A careful study of these experiments would provide useful insights on this subject. We recommend that special studies of these "action Planning" ventures in the country should be undertaken by the Multi-Level Planning Division in the Planning Commission as part of the continuing work programme. (Para 8.43)

159. People's participation, to be really meaningful, should take place at every stage of planning including preplanning, strategy setting, scheme formulation, monitoring and review and not merely at the time of plan finalisation. (Para 8.45)

160. Full benefit of the experience and special merits of voluntary agencies should be availed of wherever possible and desirable. (Para 8.47)

161. In the District Planning Bodies set up in each State, adequate representation should be provided for elected representatives, representatives of economic or occupational groups, social groups, voluntary agencies etc. as indicated in the chapter on Pre-requisites in this report. [Para 8.50(1)]

162. In order to make people's participation effectives, it is necessary to organise it at every stage of planning and

implementation including the stage of evaluation monitoring and review. [Para 8.50(2)]

163. During the pre-planning stage, involving collection of data and conduct of surveys, the local leaders of the community, teachers, students and others, as necessary, may be associated. [Para 8.50(3)]

164. At the scheme formulation stage meaningful public participation would require: (a) interaction with "people" in their village settings and with their representative organisations, (b) purposeful consultation with beneficiary groups, and (c) consultation with different categories of "people" such as landless labour, tribals, scheduled castes, artisans. [Para 8.50(4)]

165. At the stage of formulation of strategies and determination of schemes priorities the people may be involved to assist the planning team in assessing the relative response of the people to alternative strategies. The method would be to discuss in "open forums", where representatives of various local agencies at the Block and Tahsil, bubes and the representative of various interest groups could be invited to express their views. [Paras 8.50(5) 8.50(6)]

166. Certain aspects of decision-making, particularly those relating to locations of various community schemes like drinking water, school construction, feeder road construction, health centres etc. would be greatly facilitated through discussions in open assemblies in villages. [Para 8.50(7)]

167. Decision-making in regard to all vital planning matters may be done through the District Planning Bodies, in which elected representatives and various other interests are duly represented. [Para 8.50(8)]

168. Local people can be encouraged to participate in the implementation aspects of a project by: (i) making contribution of resources, (ii) assisting administration and coordination efforts, and (iii) enlisting themselves in programme activities for possible benefits. [Para 8.50(9)]

169. Involvement of people may also be secured in monitoring and evaluation of projects/programmes.

[Para 8.50(10)]

170. People's involvement may be secured with great advantage in the running, maintenance and management of various completed projects by constituting suitable organisations of people like Irrigation (wateruse) Committees, etc. [Para 8.50(11)]

171. The Working Group also recommends another aspect of public participation in local level planning by associating universities academic institutions located in the district, for various tasks of plan formulation including collection of data, conduct of surveys, analyses of data, evaluation and review of on-going schemes etc. It is recommended that the District Planning Bodies should, in this manner, enlist all available talents and skills in the district. [Para 8.50(12)]

172. The Working Group recommends that public participation in centrally directed intervention strategies in rural development, should be improved by associating people's representatives in these agencies and placing the plans prepared by them before the people's organisations, like the PRI's for clearance. [Para 8.50(13)]

173. As the scope of district Planning will be to gradually enlarge so is the scope of people's participation. For instance, to begin/with, participation through representation in District Planning Bodies may be the only feasible method of inducting popular participation. In the "stages approach" that we have visualised, this could be first stage of transition.(Para 8.51)

174. In the programmes like the Minimum Needs programme, the Special Component Plan for Scheduled Castes and the plan for the tribal people, the State Govts. Should strive to achieve some degree of public participation by involving the target groups in the decision-making as well as in the implementation process. In States, where some "free or united funds" are provided to the District Planning body for its discretionary spending public participation should be encouraged in the exercise of choice of schemes and determination of their priorities. (Para 8.52)

175. There are various beneficiary-oriented schemes forming part of the IRD Programme, in which some State have already used public participation method as a means to identify beneficiaries and to evaluate the success of this

programme. This method could be emulated by all the States in the country. (Para 8.53)

176. It is recommended that States should draw up their own appropriate strategies for public participation in tune with the sequence of decentralised development envisaged by them. (Para 8.54)

177. The detailed and rigorous kind of public participation that we have advocated running, through the phases of plan programme/project formulation, implementation, monitoring and evaluation is possible only for medium term and perspective plans. So far as Annual Plans are concerned, the nature of public participation will be confined to what obtains in the District Planning Bodies in which the public will be represented. (Para 8.55)

District Planning in North Eastern Region

178. The Working Group is of the view that while working out the new frame for district-level planning, it will be necessary that the special elements relating to the various constitutional and statutory obligations prevalent in different states as also the special feature of the tribal sub-plans should be in the nature of a comprehensive frame having a clear objective accommodating a variety of other sub-goals. (Para 9.9)

179. As regards the scope and content of the District Plan and the broad division of all plan programmes into district sector and state sector, the observations contained in the relevant chapter of this report also hold good for the North-East Region. Similarly for the distribution of divisible plan outlays among the districts, the objective mentioned viz., population, area and level of development are also equally applicable to the North-eastern Region. Taking into account the special peculiarities of this region however, we recommend that as far as possible, not less than 70% of the outlay may be assigned for population, not more than 20% for area and not less than 10% for other elements including level of backwardness. (Para 9.10)

180. The districts where the level of investments may be lower than their entitlements could be given a greater step

up in successive annual plans compared to these districts which may be better provided. (Para 9.11)

181. An ideal district plan such as the one elaborated in the chapter on Planning Methodology in this report may be difficult to carry out in these states in respect of the Seventh Five Year Plan in view of the shortage of time. The preparations for making perspective plan for each district, however, should be taken in hand immediately, so that district plans can be prepared at least from the Eighth Five Year Plan. (Para 9.12)

182. Another aspect of district level planning is to influence the on-going programmes and to take up new programmes on a year to year basis, as also for the Seventh Plan period as a whole. In this case, the first disaggregated plan for the district referred to earlier should be considered at the district level and suitably adapted to the local needs. In this regard, an incremental approach could be adopted since the on-going programmes have a logic of their own and changes should be effected with great care and caution. (Para 9.13)

183. The District Plan exercise should be started each year well ahead of the State Plan exercise so that the State Plan can be built up on the basis of the District Plans. The work on the District Plans for the following years can be started on its premise that the total outlay for the District Plan will be of the order of, Say 15% over and above the current year's figure. In accordance with the incremental approach, the District authorities may prepare their plans keeping the inter-sectoral priorities, as they are. They could however, make marginal sectoral changes upto 10%. (Para 9.14)

184. After the State Plan have been approved by the Planning Commission, the District Authorities may be indicated the Plan size and their plan proposals may be finally approved subject to such variations as may be necessary in different sectors on the basis of observations of the Planning Commission and discussions with the District level Authorities and heads of the Departments if any. This exercise could be taken up for the year 1984-85 immediately. (Para 9.16)

185. An exercise for the preparation of the Seventh Five Year Plan for each district may also be taken up. The

methodology for the preparation of the Seventh Five Year Plan for the district may be the same as suggested for the Annual Plan. (Para 9.17)

186. The Working Group, suggests that the plan outlay for each district may have a 5% nucleus fund. The nucleus fund should be available to the District Planning and Executive authorities for utilisation at their discretion. Detailed guidelines should be formulated by the States for utilisation of this fund. The nucleus fund should cover schemes upto a certain financial limit, say Rs. 50,000 or less. These programmes should not have a large recurring component. The scheme taken up, within the nucleus fund, should normally be expected to be completed within a couple of years. (Paras 9.18 & 9.19)

187. The nucleus fund could also be used for the general sector programmes suitably adopted to the local needs if necessary. The nucleus fund should not be available for subsidy programmes which should be catered in the general sectoral programmes. (Para 9.20)

188. The schemes covered under the nucleus fund could be of any description including those which may normally fall in the category of non-plan activity. It could be of any description including those which may district plan as a whole or a general scheme. It may also be used to adapt any of the ongoing programmes. (Para 9.21)

189. It is necessary that the district plan programmes should be adequately reflected in the State budgets in a formal way. It will, however be useful, if a budget supplement is prepared in which District level programmes in different sectors are consolidated and presented district-wise. (Para 9.22)

190. All District level programmes should be brought within the purview of the District Planning authority for the purposes of planning. (Para 9.23)

191. We consider the block-wise investment should be aggregated and carefully reviewed although fulfledged block-level planning exercise could be taken up at a later stage, once the process of district-level planning has been stabilised. (Para 9.25)

192. The Integrated Tribal Development Project should

be accepted as an integral part of the district level plan and, to that extent, the district plan will comprise two comprehensive plans; one for the tribal areas and the other for the non-tribal areas with mutually reinforcing elements provided in the district plan. Since our final goal is to carry planning process to the block and even a group of village level, in the Integrated Tribal Development Project areas which already have a suitable plan frame, planning at the block level may be initiated. (Para 9.26)

193. The allocation for various target group programmes from the National and the State levels should give weightage to area and population as well even when the allocation is made blockwise or districtwise. (Para 9.27)

194. The sponsoring authorities of individual programmes should accept the district the sub-district level comprehensive plans as the reference point for their programmes as well and should be satisfied with ensuring that adequate programmes have been built in for the appropriate target groups within the comprehensive plan and that the investment for that target group is not less than the contribution by the sponsoring authority. They should accept reporting of the overall programme including that for the target group for the purposes of their own programmes which may be of comparatively limited coverage. (Para 9.28)

195. In those states where the districts are of bigger size, the unit for implementation could be smaller than the district as the ITDPs or a block. In Assam the sub-division is traditionally a strong unit of administration. In some other States, on the other hand, the major implementation responsibilities may continue to be at the state-level where the district technical heads may function directly under the state department heads even though the district is taken as the unit of planning. Any ad-hoc and precipitate change in the administrative system in a hurry on *a priori* consideration just because district level planning is being initiated must be avoided at all costs. (Para 9.29)

196. The Group is of the view that as large a part of development programmes as possible envisaged under the district level plans should be assigned to the village authorities,

so that they can further consolidate their position in the changing situation and become effective units of planning and implementation in the modern system in due course. The village authorities or a group of these authorities should be provided necessary technical support for the purpose. (Para 9.30)

197. The powers for according administrative, technical and financial sanction of schemes should rest with an appropriate district-level body or officials working in the district as the case may be. While most of the powers should vest with concerned departments, the residuary powers in respect of implementation of the district plans may vest in a committee of district heads of various departments with Deputy Commissioner as the Chairman. The District Planning Authority should be responsible for monitoring of implementation of programmes in the district. (Para 9.31)

198. Keeping in view the size of the districts in the region, it may not be necessary even at a later stage to have the full-fledged technical planning unit at the district level. The Group, therefore, suggest that a strong district level planning unit may be established at the state level in all States and Units other than Assam. In Assam, the district level planning unit may be established at the regional level and function under the Divisional Commissioners. (Para 9.32)

199. The main thrust of development in each unit should determine the composition of the technical team. We recommend that the team must comprise experts in rural development planning, agriculture/horticulture/forestry, animal production/pisciculture/village industries/cooperation and social scientist. Two other experts could be added depending upon the need of each area. The North Eastern Council may obtain services of experts in rural development planning and other fields on contract basis from other areas which could be placed at the disposal of the District Planning units in the region. (Para 9.33)

200. It will be necessary to take up programmes for building up manpower for the Planning Team within the region. The work of building up manpower may be taken in earnest in the region. A Regional Centre for Multi-level

Planning may be set up under the aegis of the North Eastern Hill University. (Para 9.34 & 9.35)

Operationalising District Planning

201. District Planning process is to be conceived as as "Stages" or "Sequence" approach. This implies that decentralised development is a continuum and different stages of it are to be crossed before reaching the final stage. This is an evolutionary process and some transitional phases in this context have to be recognised. These phases are: Stage-I will be passé of "initiation" Stage-II will be one of "Limited Decentralisation" and Stage-III would represent "Final Stage". (Para 10.3)

202. In this step-by-step approach even the first step must be sufficiently backed up by political and bureaucratic will as well as effective implementation measures. Also, the planning levels above (the State Planning Boards and the Central Planning Commission) must constantly provide to the districts, technical and other assistance to stimulate and sustain this progress. (Para 10.4)

203. In order to operationalised the decentralised district planning concept in this manner from the Seventh Five Year Plan onwards, the State Governments should crystalise their thinking during 1984-85 an "approach Paper for Decentralised District Planning for the Seventh Plan 'for their States in which they should set out these Action Proposals". This Approach Paper will be considered by the Planning Commission during the Annual Plan discussions in its Working Group on District Planning. Later, this paper should be incorporated as a chapter into the Seventh Plan document of the State. Simultaneously the State should start taking several steps to implement the 'Action Proposals, so that implementation could proceed in a systematic manner in line with the action sequence envisaged. The District Planning Unit that we have proposed at the State level should undertake these jobs. (Para 10.5)

204. It is felt that the task of monitoring a better done by a smaller Committee called "Executive Committee." (Para 10.8)

205. It would become necessary to entrust the monitoring function specifically to one of the members of the planning team. (Para 10.9)

206. To look into efficient sequencing of projects/schemes at the district level during the implementation process, a separate monitoring cell in the District Planning machinery is required. A Monitoring Unit located in the State Planning Department will be its counterpart at the State level. (Para 10.9)

207. The use of modern cartographic methods through thematic maps portraying the development profile in a visually appealing manner is proving to be a useful aid for understanding plan progress. The States that are making a beginning to develop their monitoring mechanism at the district and the State levels are well advised to take note of these developments. (Para 10.10)

208. For success in decentralisation programmes it is not merely that functions, finances and powers must be deconcentrated, but also certain attitudinal behavioural and cultural conditions conducive to decentralisation have to be built up. This 'culture of decentralisation' has to grow in strength and take deep roots in the country to successfully resist the pressures for centralisation and to sustain the march towards this goal. This is of course a matter of evolution through time. But action i.e. planned and purposeful action-has to proceed much ahead of the times. (Para 10.12)

Index

■■■